Traumatized

The Story of a State Trooper

John G. Patterson

with

James R. Benn

and

Deborah L. Mandel, LPC

ISBN 978-0-615-81661-6

Cover Illustration: designed and created
by artist/tattoo artist Timothy B. Boor

Connecticut Bravery Award photo
by the Connecticut State Police

Im Traumatized LLC

Printed in the United States of America
10 9 8 7 6 5 4 3 2 1

Dedication

To my parents, Bonnie and Gary, who have taught me the importance of family and the amount of love it takes to make a family flourish.

To my sisters, Tracy, Maureen and Christine, who have always loved me for who I am and not who I've become.

To my wife, Wendy, who has dedicated her life to helping me out of the darkness and back into the light, which shines so brightly in our children's eyes.

To my three children, Amelia, Eric and Aidan, in time you will learn the reasons why daddy has acted the way he has during your childhood. Hopefully you will understand that my only goal has been to protect you all from the evil that exists in the world.

Police Officer's Prayer to Saint Michael

Saint Michael, heaven's glorious commissioner of police, who once so neatly and successfully cleared God's premises of all its undesirables, look with kindly and professional eyes on your earthly force.

Give us cool heads, stout hearts, and uncanny flair for investigation and wise judgement.

Make us the terror of burglars, the friend of children and law-abiding citizens, kind to strangers, polite to bores, strict with law-breakers and impervious to temptations.

You know, Saint Michael, from your own experiences with the devil, that the police officer's lot on earth is not always a happy one; but your sense of duty that so pleased God, your hard knocks that so surprised the devil, and your angelic self-control give us inspiration.

And when we lay down our night sticks, enroll us in your heavenly force, where we will be as proud to guard the throne of God as we have been to guard the city of all the people.

AMEN

Acknowledgments

I wish to personally acknowledge and thank the following people for their support and contributions in helping me create this book, which has greatly assisted me in healing from my Post Traumatic Stress Disorder: my wife Wendy, my children, Mia, Eric and Aidan; my parents, Bonnie and Gary, my sisters, Christine, Maureen and Tracy; and all my aunts and uncles and cousins; my friends who stuck by me during the darkest days; my co-workers who kept me focused and laughing; my co-authors, Deborah Mandel and James Benn; my therapist, Dr. Mark Hall, who helped me to understand and change what was happening inside my body, mind and soul; Timothy Boor, the artist who captured and drew the essence of all that has lived inside of me these years; and my amazingly understanding and supportive supervisor during the worst of my on-the-job times, Lieutenant John Rich. I further want to thank Jay Gaughan for keeping me alive during the first shooting incident, and Stowell Burnham, my partner, as well as Gary Inglis and Carlos "Dr. Love" Sowell, desk troopers, for keeping me alive in incident two.

I would like to thank those members of my family who have and continue to dedicate their lives to protecting others and who inspired me to become a police officer:

Vere Patterson, Hartford Police Department, Connecticut
Maureen Patterson Mckeon, Fairfax County Police
    Department, Virginia
John Bowen, Hartford Police Department, Connecticut
John Bowen Jr., Hartford Police Department, Connecticut
Barbara Moriarty Bowen, first female Sergeant in the
    Hartford Police Department, Connecticut
John Bowen 3rd, Connecticut Department of Corrections
Thomas Bowen, Chief of Bloomfield Police Department,
    Connecticut

Richard Bowen 3rd, Hartford Police Department, Connecticut
Richard Bowen 4th, Bloomfield Police Department,
    Connecticut
James Bowen, Manchester Police Department, Connecticut
Laura Buyak, Hartford Police Department, Connecticut
Joseph Buyak 3rd, Hartford Police Department, Connecticut
James Buyak, Hartford Police Department, Connecticut
Chris Doucette, Connecticut State Police
Chief John Archelaschi, Winsted Police Department
    Connecticut

I also wish to recognize the police officers with whom I've worked throughout my career who have passed on:

STATE POLICE
Don Frederick (MVA)
Cheryl Beasley (Suicide)
Don Richardson (Suicide)
Kurt Hulburt (Cancer)
Ken Hall (Line of Duty MVA)

MONTVILLE POLICE
Dennis Monahan (Cancer)
Chip Pipping (Murdered)
Joseph Sachatello (Line of Duty MVA)

My Hat goes off to you all,

John G. Patterson

Contents

Chapter 1   The bayonet..11

Chapter 2   Joe, Joe, Joe!..15

Chapter 3   What just happened?..19

Chapter 4   Jewett City in a nutshell..23

Chapter 5   ...protecting my four children
while you faced such extreme danger....................27

Chapter 6   Why me? Why again?..31

Chapter 7   Interview with Bonnie Patterson
by Deborah L. Mandel 43

Chapter 8   Déjà vu..53

Chapter 9   Forgive me Father for I have sinned 61

Chapter 10 I began having nightmares 65

Chapter 11 This is John Patterson 71

Chapter 12 Tap, tap, tappity, tap 79

Chapter 13 Interview with Dr. Mark Hall
by Deborah L. Mandel 85

Chapter 14 Crying on TV 97

Chapter 15 Shots were fired 101

Chapter 16 Isn't it true...? 103

Chapter 17 The tattoo
Interview by Deborah L. Mandel with Wendy and John Patterson.....113

Chapter 18 Brian and Sach 121

Chapter 19 Interview with Sergeant John Rich
by Deborah L. Mandel 127

Chapter 20 Let the dog maul him...139

Chapter 21 Real Stories of the Highway Patrol,
Patterson style 145

Chapter 22 Come any closer and I will blow
my fucking head off 149

Chapter 23 Return to my own land I shall not 151

Chapter 24 April and I 157
              The Retirement Poem...161

Appendix 1 Awards and Commendations 166

Appendix 2 Guidelines For Officer Involved Shootings.............168

Appendix 3 References & Resources 171
              About the Authors..172

Chapter 1

The bayonet

It was a hot August night in 1996. To be exact, it was August 10th, 10:47 p.m. It still reads in my mind like a police report, short, clipped, precise. The Troop E dispatcher sent two of us to an address in Jewett City, only minutes away. At first it was just another domestic dispute, not uncommon on a humid summer night.

As we arrived, the dispatcher told us the guy we were looking for was armed with a gun. Things changed. Trooper Keith Hoyt and I approached the house, one in a row of two-story homes set closely together, with a park across the street and a stream at their backs. There were worse places in Jewett City.

It was only a couple of steps to the front of the house. The only thing separating this house from the neighbors was a driveway of dirt, gravel and a few clumps of grass. We saw a man exit from the side door and into the driveway. There was something long in his hand. At first I thought it was a stick, about two feet long. We shined our flashlights on him and in the narrow space between the two homes, saw it was a bayonet.

"Drop the bayonet, get down on the ground!" We probably both yelled, or something close. Our weapons were drawn, flashlights on him.

"Fuck you. If you want the knife come and get it," the guy said. That I remember exactly. Then he walked back into the house as if greeting cops with a two-foot pig-sticker was a normal Saturday night event. He locked the door behind him and began screaming at the people still inside. We checked the windows and could see this individual standing in the kitchen at the rear of the house, the bayonet still in his hand.

The front door opened, and another male exited. He identified himself as Louie Lemieux, and as we searched him he told us the guy with the bayonet was Joseph Cote. Lemieux was clean, and went on to tell us that Cote was intoxicated and had been snorting cocaine. This was not good news, not for us or the people inside. Lemieux told us his girlfriend, Julie Michaelson, was still in the house, along with Cote's girlfriend, Patricia Hackett, and her son, James Hackett. Fucking great;

two women, a kid, and a coked up guy with a big knife.

As we took in this information, the front door crashed open and Julie, Patricia and James came running out, Cote at their heels with bayonet in hand. Keith and I stepped in front of the civilians, weapons drawn. At the sight of us, Cote slammed the front door shut and locked it. For a second, it seemed as if the worst had passed. Cote was alone in the house, and time was on our side. But then Patricia Hackett told us something Lemieux had not; that Joseph Cote's ten year old son Michael was in the upstairs bedroom. Damn. I immediately notified Troop E that we had an armed, barricaded subject with a possible hostage, and requested backup.

Keith and I went to the side of the house and began to talk with Cote through the kitchen window. Keith had dealt with Cote before, twice, and said it was important to keep him talking. We talked, and Cote's demeanor shifted several times. He seemed irrational, which I attributed to the influence of booze and drugs. He never loosened his grip on the bayonet, and repeatedly threatened to harm us if we tried to enter his house and arrest him.

Keith and I used any means we could to get Cote to drop the weapon and give himself up. A few times we holstered our weapons and tried to coax him out, telling him everything would be okay. He didn't bite and became more irritated when Keith and I drew our weapons again as we continued to keep the conversation going. We weren't going to endanger ourselves by not having weapons at the ready if he burst out of that door. If he wanted a confrontation, we were ready.

We heard the sirens in the distance, a reassuring sound that told us help was on the way. The back-up arrived and established a perimeter around the house. The place wasn't that big, but Keith and I hadn't been able to cover all possible exits. We watched Cote as he studied the troopers surrounding the place. Maybe that got through the fog of alcohol and coke, or maybe he had no idea what to do next, but in a few minutes he came to the door with his son Michael. He told us Michael could leave as soon as he was dressed. He had one arm around his son's shoulder, just like any dad at home with his kid. The other hand still held the bayonet.

He shut the door and a full five minutes passed. It seemed like forever. Could we count on him to keep his word? Did we have any other choice? Was it a trap, or was this Cote's way of ending the stand-off?

Finally, Joseph Cote appeared at the kitchen door, opened it and invited us in. We followed and he took a seat at the kitchen table with his son. The bayonet was lying on the table in front of him. For the first time that night, it was not in his hand. But close.

The first order of business was to get Michael out safely. We did and then placed Cote under arrest. There was no further incident. All the screaming, all the threats, all the potential for blood was gone. Police routine took over. Cote was charged with Disorderly Conduct, Threatening, Reckless Endangerment 1st Degree and Risk of Injury to a Minor. He was transported to Backus Hospital in Norwich for a psychological evaluation, after which he was brought to Troop E where he was processed and held on a cash bond. Another Saturday night in Jewett City.

After Keith and I got back to the Troop, we went over what had happened. It's a regular thing in the department, to debrief and talk about what could have gone down if things hadn't worked out. We both were clear that Cote would have been shot dead if he had made a move to attack any of the occupants of the house. Or us.

Neither of us hesitated at the thought of killing another human being, if it proved necessary. As a police officer, I was glad I hadn't wavered in my determination to use deadly force if called to. As a person, it felt strange to have such a mindset, but I knew that at some point in my career I might be faced with that choice, and I was glad I felt ready.

There was so much I didn't know.

Chapter 2

Joe, Joe, Joe!

It was Tuesday, September 3, 1996. Less than a month had passed since the incident with Joseph Cote and the bayonet. I was working the evening shift with my wing-man, Trooper Jay Gaughan. I was patrolling the towns of Lisbon and Sprague and Jay was covering the borough of Jewett City, along with the towns of Griswold and Voluntown. Jewett City was by far the busiest place to work in our troop area, so it was common for the trooper who patrolled Lisbon and Sprague to gravitate towards Jewett City for a faster response time in case of a problem. Which is what I was doing that night and for good reason. Jewett City was a haven for criminals. It is located between the cities of Norwich and Willimantic (the heroin capital of the US, according to one national news agency) and the cost of living in this one-square-mile town is a lot lower than in either of the larger cities. The majority of people who lived in Jewett City were transient, and many residents rented property. Because the Jewett City Police Department had disbanded a few years prior, the Connecticut State Police had taken over police services in the town.

Around 7:30 p.m., Jay and I were dispatched to 63 Ashland Street in Jewett City to investigate an intoxicated male who was threatening to harm himself and his sister. It was a familiar address. The Troop E desk trooper advised us the person attempting to harm himself was Joseph Cote. I filled Jay in about the previous incident and Cote's propensity for violence. Based on the last go-around, I quickly requested back-up from the Troop.

When we arrived I immediately drew my weapon and approached Cote's dirt driveway. This time, it was still light out. We could see things clearly: the narrow, closed space between the houses, kids' toys scattered in the neighbor's back yard.

We approached Cote's front door and could see him through the front window. As we walked closer, he moved to the back of the residence towards the kitchen, the place where he'd last given himself up. Walking down the driveway, we followed his movements, watching him through the windows of his house. Cote pulled a large knife from a kitchen cabinet drawer. Holding the knife in his right hand, he grabbed a beer with the other and began to drink. I knew, at that exact moment, that Jay and I were going to have to kill Joseph Cote, based on our previous interaction with him and police intuition. This knife was not going to end up lying on the kitchen table.

I told Jay what I was thinking. Jay looked at me with a blank stare for a split second, then quickly snapped back into reality. I knew it was a lot to absorb and that my previous brush with Cote prepared me for this reality. The situation hit me in the pit of my stomach and I felt physically sick at the knowledge of what was coming to pass. Cote was going to force things farther this time. Far enough so there wouldn't be a next time. My training, and perhaps my youth, allowed me to brush my feelings aside in order to concentrate on the task at hand. Focus was important. We had to think about bystanders, others who might still be in the house. Ourselves. Our loved ones who expected us to come home tonight.

Jay put his gun in his left hand and wiped the sweat off his right hand onto his uniform pants. He returned his gun to his right hand. We were both prepared for battle.

Cote was wearing khaki shorts with no shirt and again he appeared to be intoxicated or under the influence of drugs. While he was still drinking his beer, I yelled to him to put the knife down and come outside and talk to us.

"If I see one mother fucker walk into this house, I will kill him," Cote yelled, as he opened the kitchen window. I told him again to drop the knife.

"Come inside and take it from me," he yelled. Familiar words.

As Cote and I went back and forth, Jay saw a group of kids playing in the backyard of the neighboring house. He told them to get inside and stay there. As he did this, I heard Cote call his two dogs into the kitchen. He got down on one knee and hugged and kissed them, an oddly normal scene in a terribly abnormal situation. He sobbed, and said goodbye to them. Goodbye. As I heard that, a nervous calm came over me. I knew that something bad was about to happen. Not the kind of bad we see every day, but really bad. The kind of bad that never goes away. I thought about going home to my family. If getting there meant shooting and killing Cote, I felt at peace with it.

Cote opened the kitchen door and stood on the top step of his porch. He was close, only a few steps away. In the confined space between the homes, there was no room to maneuver. Jay and I retreated to the rear of the neighbor's residence in an attempt to put the safest distance between ourselves and Cote. Twenty-one feet is the proscribed distance between a police officer and someone armed with a knife. Jay and I were fewer than fifteen feet away, with nowhere else to go and still maintain visual contact.

As soon as he stepped outside I had the front sight of my Beretta 9mm fixed on his head. We're taught in the Academy to shoot twice to the body, then once to the head, the body being the bigger target. The idea is that more damage can be done to the body because of all the internal organs. But, someone could be wearing a bullet proof vest, so you take the shot to the head as well. I wasn't taking any chances. If he charged us, there would be no time for a second or third shot. I wanted to end the threat with one shot, so I kept the sight square on his head.

"You better kill me," Cote shouted. "You better shoot. Shoot, shoot!" He took another step down his porch stairs with one hand still clutching the beer, his other the knife. "You better kill me before I kill you."

Jay and I stepped backwards, distancing ourselves once more from Cote, who'd come a few feet closer. But we'd run out of driveway. With the knife in his left hand, Cote took a last swig from his beer then threw the bottle to the ground. It shattered on the stones. He switched the knife to his right hand, and ran towards us, the blade extended.

"Stop!" I yelled. Cote ignored me. There was no time for anything else. I fired my Beretta 9mm four, maybe five times. As soon as I fired my weapon, Jay fired his. Mine jammed. As I cleared the jam and reloaded with a full magazine, Cote fell face down on the gravel driveway, a few feet from us, the knife still clenched in his right hand. Everything had happened in seconds, in a confined space with houses looming above us on both sides. But in my mind, it had all happened in slow motion, as if every second were crystal clear, drawn out and burned into my memory.

Jay was yelling Joe, Joe, Joe repeatedly as we approached him, lying in the driveway of his home, dying. I saw bullet holes in the top of Cote's head and what appeared to be exit wounds on his back. I was certain I had inflicted the fatal shot to the head and I had also shot off his pinky. None of that mattered now though. Jay and I called in a Code A—shots fired—to Troop E. We needed to see if Cote was still alive and get the knife out of his hand. I knew it was doubtful that he could harm anyone at that point, but our training took over.

I checked the street and saw two teenage girls watching the drama unfold directly across from the driveway. They couldn't have been any older than thirteen or fourteen. I yelled at them to get the fuck out of there, which they did. I kicked the knife out of Cote's hand while Jay checked Cote's injuries and tried to help him until the ambulance arrived. I could hear Cote gurgling over the sounds of distant sirens, the backup I had requested when we first arrived. The distant shrill sound, drawing closer, comforted me. It was over and help was on the way. An ambulance for Cote, support for us.

Cote got the ambulance, but it did him no good. As for support, I had no clue what was about to happen. I thought the ordeal was over.

Every moment of that September evening is still with me, but what has stuck with me most over the years are Jay's screams of "Joe, Joe, Joe". Years later, chills still run through my body whenever I think about it.

Chapter 3

What just happened?

It wasn't long before back-up troopers arrived, along with the Griswold Volunteer Fire Department and the town ambulance. The EMS guys tended to Joseph Cote. The first thing the troopers did was ask Jay and me if we were okay. Of course we said we were, and they began putting crime scene tape around the area. I can't really remember who was working that evening or who showed up at the scene. Jay and I stood together in disbelief and shock. My nervous calm quickly turned into a full-fledged nightmare. Although there were only a handful of people at the crime scene, it seemed as if there were hundreds of individuals filling that small area. Everything was chaotic and surreal. My mind was racing with questions as I tried to put things together.

What just happened? Did I shoot and kill somebody? Is this for real? Am I really watching an ambulance crew performing CPR on someone I shot? What the fuck is going on?

The evening shift duty supervisor, Sergeant DiFranco, arrived at the scene. He made sure Jay and I were physically okay, and then quickly separated us. When I asked him why, he told us that Internal Affairs needed to conduct an investigation into the shooting and that he wouldn't allow Jay and me to "get our stories straight" before they arrived. That pissed me off. Jay and I had just shot and killed somebody, justifiably in our eyes, and our supervisor was throwing Internal Affairs in my face not thirty minutes in.

I thought that was bullshit. Jay and I managed to talk before the Major Crime detectives and Internal Affairs detectives arrived. Sergeant DiFranco would occasionally intervene and tell us we were "fucking things up" for ourselves. When our union representative, Bill Bowyer, showed up, I told him to keep DiFranco away from me before I slugged him. Bill stayed with us and tried to calm things down.

Bill reviewed, from a union perspective, what Jay and I should expect from the department that night and in the near future. As we stood together talking, I was replaying what had happened over and over again in my mind. I know I heard what Bill said, but I really didn't hear him. I definitely didn't understand him; there was too much noise in my head for the words to sink in.

I was twenty-six years old and a four year rookie of the Connecticut State Police. I was being investigated by my own department for committing a homicide. Although Jay and I were police officers and were acting within the parameters of the law, we did in fact commit a homicide—the killing of one person by another. That was an inescapable fact.

The Major Crime Detectives arrived and Jay and I explained exactly what had happened and where we were standing when the shooting occurred. We showed them which shell casings were ours. As we were walking through the crime scene, one of the detectives saw my magazine lying in the dirt and asked whose it was. I explained that my gun had jammed, and that I had reloaded in case Cote was still alive and able to attack us again. I saw the pool of blood on the driveway where Cote fell to the ground. I saw the knife lying next to it, and the shell casings scattered around the driveway.

Reality started slowly sinking in. It had really happened. I'd killed a man. I kept telling myself—Fuck him. He was trying to kill me, but I killed him before he could kill me.

Fuck it.

My youth and arrogance had a lot to do with this. I saw it as survival of the fittest and I had won. Maybe it was my pride, maybe relief at being alive. Maybe guilt and shame as well. Not being the only person to have shot Cote helped. I could share whatever I was feeling with Jay—spread it around so it wasn't all mine.

After explaining to the detectives what happened, Jay and I were separated again and asked to return to Troop E for a more comprehensive interview. By this time the Barracks Commander had arrived on the scene, as well as the district Major and several other high ranking individuals from our department who I didn't know, nor cared about. They too asked how Jay and I were, then immediately convened in another location, where I could hear them discussing their careers and pending promotions. These were the department members who routinely made appearances at noteworthy crime scenes to show their commitment to the Connecticut State Police, if not to the troopers who actually did the job.

To me, this was typical behavior of the Command Staff. "Hi, I'm Colonel, Captain, Major So and So. I'm in charge here and I've been a trooper for umpteen years. Oh, and by the way, how are you doing?"

I know this sounds familiar to many police officers who work for a living. That's why the only support I needed or wanted that day was from fellow troopers on the front lines. They know firsthand what sacrifices the road troopers make and how hard our jobs are, day in and day out. The Command Staff sacrifices nothing, but demands respect and admiration. To me, their cavalier attitudes deserve nothing at best, contempt at worst.

A few off-duty troopers showed up to support Jay and me and assist investigators with whatever they needed. Harold "Frenchy" French was the first to arrive. He spoke briefly with us, and then assisted the Griswold Volunteer Fire Department in their duties. Frenchy was one of a handful of troopers who fought to get one of the north patrols on a nightly basis. He knew that it was a tough place to work and that sooner or later one of us would find ourselves in this situation. It meant a lot to me that Frenchy took time out to check on me; he didn't have to be there. He had helped me through the entire process of becoming a trooper and I looked up to him. He was, and will always be, a model trooper, and as long as I had fellow officers at the scene like Frenchy, I felt I would be fine.

Before we left the scene, a detective asked us for our weapons as they were needed as evidence in the investigation. We turned them over, but this left us unarmed as we were driven back to Troop E. We were given no replacement guns for the twenty-mile ride to the Troop. Obviously the Department did not care if we might need a weapon during this time. Thank God nothing else happened that night.

I can't remember who drove me back to the barracks. During the ride I began to think about who I needed to call. Most importantly I wanted to call my parents and my fiancée Wendy to let them know I was alive and okay. When we arrived at the barracks I was told that a local Police Officer had already driven over to see my parents and Wendy and had told them what had happened and that I was unhurt. As soon as possible I called my parents and asked my father to drive to my house to check on Wendy. After describing the events of the evening, and reassuring him that I was really fine, my father agreed to get Wendy and drive her back to his house. A short time later I called Wendy and told her that Jay and I were okay and that I'd meet her at my parents' house as soon as I could, which probably wouldn't be for several hours.

Detectives interviewed Jay and me separately and then asked us to write detailed reports about the shooting. When we completed our reports, Jay and I talked about what had happened to us and concluded that our reports were eerily similar. We both knew we had done things by the book and neither of us was worried about the criminal investigation or the Internal Affairs investigation. Around midnight, four and a half long hours after the shootings, we were finally given permission to go home. The Barracks Commander, Lieutenant Constantine, told us to take the next day off but to come in to take care of some reports. We were placed on administrative leave until further notice.

At some point during the evening, Joseph Buyak, my cousin and a Hartford Police Officer, had called the barracks and I had spoken with him briefly. I was glad to hear from Joey. I looked up to him as a person and as a police officer. He always put me at ease. He told me that he would drive to Troop E to pick me up and bring me home. When he showed up, instead of being able to leave, Jay and I were told by the Detectives to return to 63 Ashland Street to answer a few more questions. Joey drove me to the scene and Jay drove separately. My memory is a little foggy about that time, but I think they wanted to know how close Cote was to us when we shot him and which shell casings were ours. We did the best we could to answer their questions and then, thankfully, we were allowed to go home.

On the drive down to my parents' house Joey and I talked about how and why the shooting occurred and what had happened when Jay and I got back to the barracks. Having that conversation was helpful. When we arrived, I was greeted by my crying mother, my father, and Wendy. My cousin, John Bowen, who has always been a brother to me, was also waiting at my parents. We talked for a while, then everyone went to bed. Wendy asked me if I would be able to fall asleep and I replied yes.

Wendy then said something simple, profound and insightful. "I knew you carried a gun, but I never thought you would have to use it."

That was exactly how I felt. Police officers carry a gun, but few fully realize the possibility that they may have to use it. Years later, that statement still rings true. I knew I carried a gun for a living, but I never believed I would use it to take the life of another human being. But it had happened. A once-in-a-lifetime occurrence. It was over.

Or so I thought.

Chapter 4

Jewett City in a nutshell

W ednesday morning, September 4, 1996, Wendy and I went about our day as if nothing out of the ordinary had happened the night before. I called Jay, but got no answer. Usually when he worked evenings he watched television after his shift, often until four o'clock in the morning, and slept in until after noon. But I thought he might have gotten up earlier that morning because of what we had gone through. Then around nine o'clock I began to get phone calls from my family, friends and coworkers. Everyone was interested in what happened, but more importantly, they were genuinely concerned about my well-being, as well as Wendy's. After I had spoken with a few of the callers, I retrieved the local paper, The New London Day, from my front step. There was a brief article about the shooting. It didn't mention my name or Jay's, for which I was grateful. I could care less what people had to say about me, but I didn't want my parents to be bombarded at work with questions about what I had done.

The newspaper account stated that two state troopers had shot an armed suspect in Jewett City and that the incident was under investigation. State Police spokesman Dale Hourigan was quoted as saying that the troopers were being "interviewed and counseled" on Tuesday night and that our names would not be made public until Thursday. At the time, our department had no guidelines or departmental procedures for dealing with the emotional repercussions for anyone who had been involved in a shooting and no one in our department had offered Jay or me any type of counseling at all. It was laughable that the department had the audacity to put that statement in the paper. Then again, a department can't get fired for lying; only a trooper can. The only support I received was from my family, my friends, and my fellow police officers.

A few hours later Joey Buyak called and asked me if he could come down and take me out to lunch. He brought his siblings, Jimmy and Laura, and our cousin Ricky Bowen along. Jimmy was a Patrolman for the Hartford Police Department, Laura was a detective for the Department and Ricky was a cop in Windsor Locks. It felt right. We went to lunch and talked about what had happened and joked about how I was the first one in our family to shoot somebody in the line of duty. This seemed even more absurd because I worked in the boonies and they worked in big cities. We had a few drinks and shared a few laughs about Jewett City. I gave then my opinion on Jewett City; it was a dump, the people dressed like they were stuck in the 1980s and there was probably more crime per capita there than any place in the state or maybe even in the nation.

I told them about one evening shift during the past summer, when my partner Keith Hoyt and I were dispatched to an accident with injuries at the main intersection in town. Within five minutes of arriving at the scene, Keith and I were re-dispatched to an overdose about fifty yards away. We ran to that scene, and found the overdose victim/asshole collapsed in the doorway of the apartment building with the needle still stuck in his arm. While providing medical assistance to him, the North Patrol was sent to an active domestic dispute. This sort of shit happened every night in the summer for a three or four year stretch.

Here's Jewett City in a nutshell. One day, driving my cruiser down Ashland Street, I saw a guy walking his eighty pound dog on a leash. As I passed the two of them, the dog squatted and took a shit in the middle of the sidewalk. I watched in my rear view mirror as the guy just walked away with the dog, not bothering to pick up that big ole pile of shit. I just laughed. One day I got dispatched to an apartment on North Main Street because the owner of the apartment building found something disturbing when he was cleaning it for the new tenants. I arrived on the scene and the owner hands me a small Elio's Frozen Pizza box with three dead, frozen kittens, stuck together in it. I looked at this guy like "Are you fucking kidding me?" What do you want me to do with these things? Pizza anyone?

That sums up the mentality of a lot of Jewett City's fine citizens. They should be living in a tent in the middle of Appalachia. One Halloween I got sent to an apartment building on South Main Street to investigate a woman who was placing head stones in front of the building as decorations. I got out of my car and started walking towards what I thought were fake headstones. Nope. Little Miss Freak Show had driven down the street a half hour earlier and found two headstones from babies that died in the 1800s and decided to steal them and place them in front of her apartment building for Halloween. Jerry Springer would have had a field day in Jewett City. He could host a different fucked up show every day of the week for at least a month. Two of Connecticut's Death Row inmates were from Jewett City. Serial killer Michael Ross, who was put to death for the murder of eight young women in the 1980s, and Terry Johnson, the killer of Connecticut Trooper Russel Bagshaw both lived on the outskirts of town. If I ever opened up a business in Jewett City, it would be a Laundromat/bar that sold video games, because most people in town didn't own a washer and dryer and would rather sit home and drink and play video games than get a job.

I told all this to Joey, Jimmy, Laura and Ricky. I didn't learn until later that my aunt, Barbara Moriarty Bowen, had actually been the first uniformed family member to shoot and kill someone in the line of duty.

Jay and I got together later in the day. He came down to my house and we hung out for a while. We talked about what had happened the night before, and how we'd both slept soundly despite it. Neither of us had any second thoughts or regrets about what we'd done. We slept like babies that night as well.

The following day—Thursday—we went into work to catch up with our reports. Throughout the day numerous people stopped in to see how we were doing and asked if we needed anything. Not a single one of them was from our Command Staff. Jay and I discussed the shooting a little, but not as much as I would have thought, given the intensity of the situation. It almost felt like a regular day at the job until Lieutenant Constantine informed us we would have to work desk duty at the Troop until the Internal Affairs' and the State's Attorney's investigations were completed. Our department manager never asked Jay or me where we would like to work, or what we wanted to do during the investigations. He had no idea how long it would take until we were cleared by our agency to return to our normal duties. This was the thanks Jay and I got for doing our jobs. Troop E was the busiest barracks in the state and the last thing anyone wanted to do was work the desk. Our Troop had no 911 dispatchers, so not only did the desk trooper have to monitor the police radio, they had to answer regular service calls as well as 911 emergencies. It was utter chaos—it was a nightmare and I hated it. Jay and I both felt that working the desk was a punishment for what we had done in the line of duty.

A lengthy article appeared in The Day newspaper (New London, CT) that Thursday morning about Joseph Cote and the shooting. The reporter described Cote's drug and alcohol problems, and outlined the circumstances leading to Jay's and my being called to his house and the ensuing shooting. The only part of the article that bothered me was comments made by one of Cote's friends. He criticized us for shooting Cote instead of subduing him. This friend described Cote as a "little guy, maybe 5'10' and staggering drunk." He went on to state "Don't tell me the only option these troopers had was to shoot him."

Although Cote was short at 5"8", he weighed 213 pounds and he worked construction. Apparently Jay and I should have disregarded the large knife that Cote was wielding as he attacked us, as well as the fact that he was under the influence of alcohol and mind-altering drugs. I've wrestled with men and women who were under the influence of drugs who weighed 120 pounds and who put up a decent fight when I tried to arrest them. I wasn't about to take my chances with Cote while he was armed. Maybe this friend thought Jay and I could have shot the knife out of his hand while he was running full speed at us, like they do in the movies. If that were the case, and we'd tried that, I'm sure either Jay or I wouldn't be here right now. These idiotic statements pissed me off. I hoped that the people who read the article were intelligent enough to realize that disarming an aggressive, knife wielding man on drugs was extremely dangerous if not impossible.

Chapter 5

...protecting my four children
while you faced such extreme danger

A few days after the shooting we received a letter. It was from Laurie Sorder, the woman who lived next door to the Cote residence. This letter provided me a moment of welcome kindness in an otherwise difficult time. I was happy that Ms. Sorder felt moved to write down her feelings and send them to Jay and me. She, at least, believed that we had done the right thing to protect ourselves as well as others around us. It helped to have someone in our corner when it felt like we were being penalized by our own department. While Command Staff ignored us and their spokesman lied to the media about our receiving counseling, this young mother lifted our spirits with her letter.

September 6, 1996

> *Dear Officers Gaughn and Patterson:*
> *I am writing to thank you for protecting myself and my children during the tragic episode which occurred on September 3, 1996, at 63 Ashland Street in Jewett City. My children, unaware of the danger which faced them on that evening, went out to play on their trampoline in our backyard, which was approximately thirty feet from where you were situated. I do not know which officer told them to get inside. I witnessed one officer attempting to calm Mr. Cote, while the other officer warned my children by demanding that they go inside our home. When I attempted to return to my home from our backyard a moment later I was also motioned to get inside.*
> *I would like to commend you for your courage and dedication to the safety of innocent people during this extremely stressful situation. I cannot thank you enough for protecting my four children while you faced such extreme danger.*
> *I have given my statement regarding what I saw and heard that evening. I am thoroughly convinced that you did what was necessary, and I would like to express my sympathy to you for your unfortunate experience.*

Sincerely, Lori Sorder

When I became the Jewett City Resident Trooper a few years later, I stopped by her house and thanked her personally for writing to us.

A second event that helped with my healing from the Cote shooting occurred a few years later, during an evening shift I was dispatched to an accident on the outskirts of town. A teenage driver had lost control of his vehicle around a sharp curve and flipped the car onto someone's lawn. After arriving at the scene and determining that there were only minor injuries, I began speaking with the local residents. While doing so, a woman came up to me and ever so politely informed me that she was Joseph Cote's sister and that the car was resting on their father's lawn. The woman said that she harbored no ill will against me for killing her brother but she did ask me if someone else could investigate the accident because her father would become upset and angry if he knew that I was there. After telling her I was sorry for causing her family so much pain, I told her that I would gladly have another trooper respond to the scene and take over. I radioed Keith and explained to him what had happened. He agreed to take over the investigation, and I drove away from the Cote house, never to have any contact with the family again. To this day I still think about the way Cote's sister treated me. Knowing that I had killed her brother, she still made the effort to interact with me in an empathetic way. She didn't demand an explanation or an apology for my actions, but treated me with compassion.

In direct opposition to the support we received from some people, our department's handling of the shooting was appalling. A major flaw was their lack of support. Their only response to the media, when asked, was that the incident was under investigation, despite the fact that the Command Staff knew that the shooting was justified. They didn't have either the decency or the balls to tell the public that what we did was right and that the Connecticut State Police stood behind their police officers. The media and the citizens of the state were questioning our integrity as police officers and our Command Staff refused to stand up for us. This was one of the many reasons why I became so disillusioned with the department and held 99% of the Command Staff in disdain. They just left us hanging out there, and I had to wonder if they were more worried about the possible effect on their careers than us, their fellow troopers.

For the next three months, Jay and I worked different shifts as the desk trooper. I was so stressed out having to deal with other people's problems and complaints that I wanted to kill someone, no pun intended. This was the first time in my career that I actually hated to go to work. I despised answering telephones and being a dispatcher. I had always looked at the troopers who took the desk as being unmotivated and unwilling to do real police work. They were the pussies who would take ten minutes to drive two miles for a fight or take the long way to an accident scene or a burglary so they didn't have to do any paperwork. I hated troopers who called themselves cops and showed up at work to collect a paycheck for doing nothing and were proud of it. I called them retired on duty, and there were quite a few officers who fit that description. Being forced to work as the desk trooper felt like a slap in the face. I always took pride in how I handled myself on the road. Whenever a hot call came in—a large fight or a violent domestic—I wanted to be the first one there. If it was on my patrol I was the first one there, and if it wasn't, I would either backup the responding troopers, or at least start driving their way. When I was on patrol I didn't wait for calls. I looked for work. If I wasn't trying to serve arrest warrants, I would be stopping cars looking for narcotics and other illicit stuff. I hated sitting around doing nothing. I found the exile to a desk job so stressful that I used more sick time and vacation days during those months than I had during any other three month period in my previous four years of employment.

Until we were cleared by the State's Attorney's Office and Internal Affairs on December 3, 1996, a full three months after the shooting, no one from my department asked me if I needed any help, if I wanted to work in any other capacity at the barracks, or whether I needed any time off. Nothing from State Police management.

At one point, Jay and I sought out our department's shrink of our own accord. During our session he seemed more focused on telling us how we should feel than asking us how we felt. It was pointless, and Jay and I decided the shrink was crazy and we were fine emotionally. We never went back.

Once we were cleared, Jay and I were able to return to some kind of normalcy in our lives. We continued to work in the same towns that we had worked in prior to the shooting and we both continued to be aggressive police officers. While we had been very good friends before the shooting, we became best friends in the aftermath. We continued to work together and hang out together for the next two years, going on ski trips to great places like Innsbruck, Lake Tahoe, Whistler Mountain in Canada and Breckinridge in Colorado. We'd go to dinner, Red Sox games, out drinking, or to each others' houses, often with Wendy. I was the best man at his wedding. Looking back, I realize I was traveling to get away from my life, and Jay was right there with me.

During that time I began to notice changes in my short-term memory. It generally happened during conversations with people I didn't really know. I would forget their names, or I wouldn't remember what we had talked about. Initially I thought I was tuning people out because the conversation didn't have anything to do with me or didn't interest me. Over time this became more noticeable. I had a handful of nightmares related to the shooting, but in general everything seemed to be going fine in both my personal and professional life.

Wendy and I were married in May 1997. Later that year Jay and I were given the Courage of Connecticut Award which is sponsored by the Connecticut Coalition of Police Officers to recognize fellow officers that have willingly placed themselves in life threatening situations and survived with honor. The recipients generally have been involved in gun battles, shot, stabbed, hit with vehicles or have been directly and personally involved in the use of force. It is an award given by rank and file officers, not the management brass.

We were also recognized by TOP COPS in Washington D.C., which is sponsored by The National Association of Police Officers to pay tribute to outstanding law enforcement officers from across the country for actions above and beyond the call of duty. TOP COPS awardees are nominated by their fellow officers for outstanding service during the preceding calendar year and one officer is chosen from each state and U.S. territory. The officers are then ranked and the top ten winners are flown to Washington for the awards ceremony. We didn't win but went to the ceremony in D.C. to support our fellow officers. We felt honored by the recognition of our fellow officers, as well as the support from friends and family. By the fall of 1997, I believed that the shooting was behind me and that as a newly married man, honored by my peers for my actions, I would go back to life as usual on the beat.

Life would never again be as usual. How much so, I had no idea.

Chapter 6

Why me? Why again?

It was Sunday, December 27, 1998. Twenty-seven months after the Jewett City shooting, nineteen months after getting married and five weeks after the birth of my first child, Amelia.

On that cold day a chain of events began to unfold in the northern part of the state, events that insured my life would not emerge unscathed from encounters with criminal violence.

Stanley Megos was at his home at 245 Westford Road in Eastford, Connecticut with two friends, Andrew Licata and Joseph Parsons. Parsons had been living with Megos for a week. On that day, Megos and Parsons began to argue when Megos confronted him about having drunk his alcohol. A short time later, Megos noticed his bedroom door had been broken down. Looking for Parsons, he found him hiding in the downstairs bathroom with a revolver and shotgun he had stolen from the bedroom. When Megos entered the bathroom Parsons pointed the revolver at his head. Knowing the gun was loaded, Megos asked Parsons to point it away from him. Parsons did, but placed the revolver first against his ear and then into his mouth.

Megos unsuccessfully tried to talk Parsons into putting the guns down. Finally, Parsons asked Megos to call his friend, Tom, a nine and a half year veteran of the Greenwich, Connecticut Police Department. Parsons and Tom had been friends for twenty-four years; he had been Tom's best man at his wedding. Relieved that he might get some help with this increasingly volatile situation, Megos called Tom at 3:15 pm at his home.

Parsons was clearly intoxicated when he got on the phone with Tom. He rambled on about restraining orders and being wanted by the Orange Police Department. Parsons asked Tom to contact the Orange Department to see if there was a warrant out for him, and to tell them that if so, he would turn himself in. Parsons told Tom where he was and gave him the address. Tom quickly called the Orange Police and confirmed there was an arrest warrant out for Parsons. He contacted Parsons and told him the bond was $5,000. Parsons said he would drive to Orange and turn himself in. Tom told Parsons that he was too drunk to drive and they argued about it for a little while. Tom knew Parsons wouldn't turn himself in, so he contacted the Orange Police to let them know Parson's whereabouts. He informed them of Parsons' history of heavy drinking and his propensity to get into trouble when he was intoxicated. Tom thought it would be best to have Joe picked up in Eastford, so he drove to work and contacted Troop D in Danielson to let them know what was going on. He explained to the Troop D desk trooper that Joe was wanted by the Orange Police Department and that he needed to be picked up in Eastford. He warned the desk trooper that Joe got violent when he drank and that he had weapons in his possession.

While he was at headquarters, Tom got a phone call from his wife who had just received a call at home from Stan Megos, who wanted a call back. When Tom called Stan he learned that Parsons had taken Megos' guns, and was saying things like "it was all hopeless" and "it was all over". Tom asked Stan to give Joe Parsons the phone and told Joe to unload the guns and give them to Stan. Stan got back on the phone and when Tom asked if Joe had unloaded the guns, Stan said no. Tom then heard Stan say to Joe, "Don't point the gun at me!" Stan then told Tom that Joe had put the cocked gun in his mouth. While he still had Stan on the line, Tom had his Sergeant call Troop D and relay the information to the responding officers. Tom told Stan not to tell Joe that the State Police were on the way. After questioning Stan as to what type of weapons Joe had in his possession—to which Stan responded that he had a .38 and a shotgun—Tom requested that Stan leave the phone off the hook so he could continue to monitor what was happening. Tom told Stan to get out of the house with his friend. As soon as Joe went upstairs, Stan and Andrew Licata left the house and drove around. When they returned home a short while later, they noticed that Parsons had left in his girlfriend's vehicle, a gray Chevy Lumina with CT registration 767MMR. When the troopers arrived they gave them the information about the stolen vehicle. A heavily armed and intoxicated man, wanted by the police, was on the road.

That day I was working the evening shift in Jewett City, where I was now the Resident State Trooper. I began my shift as usual by doing patrol checks of the business areas and trouble spots. I figured the shift would be quiet and go by quickly because of the holidays and the fact that criminals do not like to expose themselves to extremely cold weather. After patrolling for about an hour, I drove back to my office and met with my wing-man and wing-woman, Troopers Stowell Burnham and Kerry Perez. Burnham was working in the towns of Griswold and Voluntown and Perez was covering Lisbon and Sprague. We were all hoping to have an uneventful evening so we could get some of our late reports done.

At approximately 5:45 pm, Natalie Bessios and April Paris were driving on I-395 in Plainfield when they observed a gray colored Chevy Lumina driving erratically in front of them. They followed the vehicle off the highway at Exit 87 and into a gas station where they observed the operator get out of his vehicle and urinate on the ground near the gas pumps. Natalie used a pay phone to call 911 and reported the incident. She provided Troop D a description of the vehicle, a gray Chevy Lumina with the license plate, 767MMR. Troop D promptly relayed the information to Troop E.

Off-duty Plainfield Police Officer Michael Suprenant and passenger Lee Yaworski were traveling south on I-395, about 5:55 pm, when they observed the gray colored vehicle being driven erratically ahead of them. When drivers attempted to pass the car, the operator made hand gestures out of his driver's side window, moved his vehicle into the left lane, and slowed down, forcing the passing vehicle to come up on his rear. Suprenant believed the driver was attempting to provoke a confrontation with another driver. As they approached Exit 85, the gray vehicle struck the cement curb off of the left shoulder with his wheels and rims, causing sparks to fly from the vehicle. As it approached the Exit 85 south bound ramp, the operator maneuvered his vehicle into the off ramp lane. As he got closer to the actual ramp, he suddenly swerved back into the right lane of I-395 and continued south on the highway. As he drove past the ramp, Suprenant noticed two cruisers with their lights activated at the end of the ramp and assumed the police were conducting seat belt enforcement inspections. He continued to follow the gray vehicle in order to stop the operator himself, or get to a phone to inform the police.

Shortly before 6:00 p.m. the Troop E Desk Trooper, Carlos Sowell, put out a broadcast over the state police radio to be on the lookout for a gray Chevy Lumina bearing CT 767MMR plates. The driver of the car was Joseph Parsons. He was armed with a shotgun and had threatened to do harm to any police officer who tried to stop him. Trooper Sowell

also said Parsons had been involved in an accident in the town of Plainfield, just north of Griswold. So much for an uneventful evening of
catching up on reports.

With Suprenant closely following, the Lumina turned off the
highway at Exit 84, and took a right onto Route 12 North at the bottom
of the ramp, without stopping at the stop sign. While traveling north
on Route 12, Parsons crossed over the centerline, almost causing a head
on collision with a south-bound vehicle. The car came to a complete
stop in the middle of the roadway and Parsons stuck his middle finger
out of his side window. He then pulled into the McDonald's parking
lot. Suprenant followed, and when Parsons parked his Lumina sideways
on the north side of the restaurant, Suprenant went up to his car and
asked him for directions to the casino. While Suprenant was distracting
Parsons, Lee Yaworski, Suprenant's passenger, used the pay phone at
McDonalds and called 911.

After learning that the suspects vehicle was spotted in the area
Stowell and I ran out of the office. As we were leaving the parking lot
we learned the suspect was at the McDonald's in Lisbon, only 1.5 miles
away. As we were responding via lights and sirens, Sergeant Lynch
advised us that he had received a call stating that the vehicle in question
was on the north side of the McDonalds Restaurant.

Meanwhile Suprenant, while engaging Parsons with idle conversation, could smell the alcohol on his breath. Parsons kept passing out.
When he came to, he would yell "fuck you" or "go fuck yourself" at
Suprenant. Suddenly he began fumbling around on the passenger side
of the car and Lee Yaworski yelled that Parsons had a gun. Suprenant
took cover, and Parsons sped off, his vehicle striking a Chevy Blazer
parked in the lot.

Just at that moment I pulled into the parking lot. I had been traveling south on Route 12 directly in front of Trooper Stowell Burnham's
cruiser and I drove to the right (north) side of the restaurant, while
Stowell drove to the left. As I neared the side of the building I observed
the Chevy Lumina with the Connecticut registration 767MMR take
off. I followed the gray vehicle around the rear of the building and
observed damage to the front passenger side of the vehicle, which I
assumed was caused when the operator was involved in the accident in
Plainfield earlier in the afternoon. I advised Stowell to block the Lumina's path so Parsons wouldn't be able to drive around his cruiser and

behind the building and make it back out onto Rout 12 or I-395. I was hoping Stowell and I would be able to conduct a felony stop behind the restaurant where there were no people. That way, if things went horribly wrong, everyone inside the restaurant and in the parking lot would be safe from any potential gunfire.

Unfortunately, things didn't work out as I had hoped. When Stowell blocked the Lumina's path with his cruiser, Parsons drove his car over a curb and into the McDonald's Drive Thru lane in an effort to escape. I immediately drove my cruiser around Stowell's and proceeded to the south side of the building where I could clearly see the Lumina and Parsons. I parked my cruiser at a 45 degree angle toward the Drive Thru lane and the Lumina. There was a van waiting to pick up food at the Drive Thru window. As soon as the Lumina came to a stop, Parsons began rocking back and forth in his seat. His expression reminded me of the look Jack Nicholson's character had in The Shining when his wife was trying to keep him away from her with a baseball bat as he was walking up the stairs in the hotel toward her. It was that same dark and evil expression and sarcastic smile. At that moment my intuition told me things were going to turn violent. Quickly. In a flash multiple thoughts raced through my mind; he had pointed a gun at Megos; he had placed a gun in his mouth; he had said he would shoot any police that came near him; his rocking; the odd expression on his face; reflections of my first shooting. I just knew.

Parsons continued to rock back and forth in his seat as I exited my cruiser and ran up a small embankment toward the passenger side of the Lumina. I had my .40 caliber Sig Sauer in my right hand and a flashlight in my left hand. Parsons began to drive his vehicle up on the left curb of the lane, towards the van that was stopped at the window. I thought his vehicle actually struck the side of the restaurant. By this point I had tunnel vision and was concentrating all my efforts on apprehending Parsons as quickly as possible. I didn't know where my wing-man Stowell or my wing-woman Kerry were. I figured Stowell and his K-9, Blizzard, would be seconds behind me, but I wasn't even sure if Kerry had left the Jewett City Office yet. As I got to the top of the embankment, Parsons stopped his vehicle and removed his right hand from the steering wheel, reaching toward the passenger area of the car. I yelled at him repeatedly to show me his hands. I used my flashlight to smash out the passenger side window of the Lumina so I could see what he was reaching for. It was the first time in my career that I was actually able to smash out a vehicle's window, and I recall being surprised it had worked.

I expected to see a shotgun in the front passenger seat because of the earlier radio broadcast, but there was no shotgun. Now I didn't know what to expect or what kind of weapon Parsons actually had. As I reached into the car to grab Parsons and remove him from the vehicle, he grabbed a silver-plated .38 revolver from the space between the center console and front passenger seat and raised it toward me, pointed it at my head and told me to "get the fuck out of here". I leaned away from his line of fire behind the passenger side door jamb and blindly fired my weapon in his direction. The muzzles of our guns were almost touching. As I was shooting, I retreated down the embankment, although I didn't realize that I had until later. I saw Stowell out of the corner of my eye, crouched down to the rear of Parsons' vehicle, holding Blizzard by his leash. I yelled to Stowell that Parsons had a gun.

From my position I could see Parsons rocking back and forth. I was horrified and shocked because it appeared Parsons was not injured and I had missed him with the first three or four shots I took. I felt like I was going crazy because I had been shooting my whole life and I was an excellent shot. Luckily, I had kept my front sight on Parsons' head and as he raised his right arm and pointed his revolver directly at me, I squeezed off one more round, striking him just below and slightly behind his right ear. Everything was happening in slow motion. I saw the bullet strike Parsons' head, causing it to flop to the side. I saw his blood pouring out of the bullet wound as if it was water coming out of a fountain. In the heat of the moment, I didn't know if Parsons had gotten off any rounds. I later learned investigators found empty shell casings in his revolver and tests determined that he had indeed fired his gun.

The next thing I remember was reaching into my cruiser and yelling into the radio that I needed an ambulance and a supervisor as soon as possible because I had shot the suspect in the head. I heard sirens and people screaming, and soon everybody started to show up. I saw Kerry and two other troopers from the Traffic Unit; Trooper Guerra, an academy classmate of mine, and Trooper First Class Prouty. I vividly remember approaching the vehicle with Kerry, Guerra and Prouty to make sure Parsons was incapacitated and couldn't harm anyone.

After clearing Parsons' car, I headed toward Sergeant Jack Hardell's vehicle. Before I made it all the way to his car I realized I was crying. Why me? Why again? I stood by his vehicle helpless, as the Sergeant hugged and consoled me. I later came to understand that I was crying because I hadn't really dealt with the trauma I'd suffered from the first shooting and everything hit me at once. It was like a giant slap in the face. I was falling apart.

Why me? Why again? I asked Jack repeatedly. I can't remember what if anything he replied, but I was glad he was there when I needed him. If he hadn't been there at that exact moment, I seriously think I might have had a nervous breakdown at the scene. Jack brought me to his cruiser, and while we were there Trooper Guerra came up and told Jack that he had Parsons' gun, which he had found on the front passenger seat. I had already told both of them that the gun was a silver plated snub-nosed .38 caliber revolver. I knew that I had seen the gun in Parsons' hand, but I needed reassurance from somebody that what I had seen was real. Trooper Guerra assured me that the gun I described to him was the same gun he had removed from Parsons' vehicle. When he held it up and showed Jack, I could see that the gun he held in his hands was the same gun I'd had pointed in my face.

Parsons had taken something else with him in the car that night; a picture of himself which he'd stuck in the dashboard. It was a photograph of him in a black tank top, arms extended, firing a pistol. I believe that's how he planned for the night to end.

When I finally got out of Jack's car, I began to walk around the scene yelling things like what the fuck - you mother fucker - you fucking cock-sucker. I didn't care who was around or who could hear me. From the outside it might have looked like I had Tourette's Syndrome. I was that pissed off. I was angry at Parsons for putting me in this situation again. During my tirade I saw Stowell walking around his cruiser, so I walked over to him and asked if he was okay. I put my hand on his shoulder to let him know that I was okay. He walked away from me with tears in his eyes. I've been friends with Stowell my whole life and I had never seen him as emotional as he was that night—he's not an emotional guy. But at that instant, without having to say anything out loud, we both knew everything was okay. We were alive and the bad guy was dead.

Soon an ambulance arrived on the scene and for some unknown reason they tried to resuscitate Parsons. I couldn't understand why; he had been dead for some time. Then everyone and their brother who was working the evening shift at Troop E and Troop D arrived at the scene to check things out and make sure Stowell and I were okay. They were especially concerned because they knew I had shot and killed another armed suspect two years earlier in Jewett City.

As soon as my sergeant, Gene Labonte, arrived on the scene, I was asked to sit in his cruiser until it was time to leave. Once again I was separated from the other troopers to keep from jeopardizing the investigation. Internal Affairs didn't like it when troopers talked to each other before their holier than thou investigators had spoken with you. I really didn't care. I knew that what I had done was justified and that Stowell was okay. I really didn't care about anyone else.

While I was waiting in Gene's car I kept replaying what had happened over and over in my mind. Because of my previous situation, I knew that I would be interviewed by the Major Crime Investigators and would need to provide them with a written statement about what I had done, step by step. But the first thing I wanted to do when I got back to the barracks was to call my parents and my wife. I wanted to tell them what had happened and I needed to reassure them that Stowell and I were okay. I didn't want them to find out what had happened through the news media. At no point during the evening did I give a thought to any repercussions that might come from being involved in another shooting.

Prior to leaving the scene and returning to the barracks, my weapon was taken from me for investigative purposes. This time the department provided me with a gun for the ride back. I was glad not to have a repeat of my first shooting when they took our weapons and forced us to drive back to the barracks unarmed, apparently believing that criminals stop committing crimes in other areas when something of this nature takes place. I don't remember what Gene and I talked about on the way to the barracks. I had so much going on in my head that everything was a blur. It was like being driven home after a night of drinking, with your head tilted to one side, staring blankly out the window at the sky passing by.

When we arrived at the barracks, I immediately thanked the Desk Troopers, Carlos Sowell and Gary Inglis, for performing their jobs so well, and saving our lives. They had passed on the information they received from Troop D quickly and with great detail, letting us know that Joseph Parsons was armed and that he threatened to harm any police officers who attempted to stop him. They had given a description of the vehicle he was driving and updated information on his location in a timely manner. If we didn't know that Parsons was armed, things might have turned out differently.

I asked Carlos to contact Jay Gaughan at the Casino Unit and ask him to get over to Troop E as quickly as possible. Because we had gone through the first shooting together, he was the only person who would know what I was experiencing and I needed his support, both professionally and personally, before I spoke to anyone, even my wife or parents. Meanwhile, I accompanied Sergeant Labonte into his office to make some phone calls. The first person I called was my Union Representative, Kenneth Washburn. I've known Kenny my entire career and was very friendly with him outside of work. As soon as he answered the phone I told him that I had just shot and killed an armed person at the McDonald's in Lisbon. Kenny laughed, said "fuck you" and hung up on me. Laughing, I told Gene that the bastard didn't believe me and had hung up! Gene laughed too and asked me if I wanted him to call Kenny back. I said no, and called Kenny myself. It took me a few minutes to convince Kenny, but once he realized I wasn't fucking around, he told me not to talk to anyone until he got there.

I was relieved when Jay arrived. I hugged him the moment he walked into my Sergeant's office. I was never so happy to see anyone. I needed his reassurance that everything was going to be okay. Against the Connecticut State Police Internal Affairs protocol, I told him what had happened. Not because he wanted to hear it, but because I needed to say the words out loud to someone who implicitly understood. At that moment I was taking care of myself, and I didn't give a fuck about the department regulations.

I called my mother and father at home and told them what had happened. I asked my dad if he would drive to my house and tell Wendy for me. My first child, Amelia, had been born only five weeks earlier and I didn't want to tell Wendy this news on the telephone and overly upset her. After the last shooting a Sergeant at the barracks had sent a local officer to my house to give Wendy the news, and I knew the last thing my wife wanted to see was a police officer showing up at her door unannounced, especially while taking care of an infant. That's every police spouse's worst nightmare. It usually means their husband or wife is dead and won't ever be coming home again. I wanted my dad to tell Wendy so she wouldn't have to go through that. I reassured my dad that

I was okay, and he agreed to tell Wendy what had happened.

Over the next couple of hours, people I knew from work called me or came to see me at the barracks to ask if I was okay or if I needed anything. The Lieutenant from my barracks stopped by to make sure I was okay and I think the District Major came to the Troop to check on me. A few other Connecticut State Police big wigs showed up and did their two or three second 'greet and stare' routine and then left. Once again, I did not have the feeling they cared about me or what I had just gone through, rather they wanted to spend enough time at the barracks so that their subordinates could say they had been there. Stowell and I managed to find a spot in the back corner of the secretary's office to quickly go over what had happened at the scene.

As I was waiting to be interviewed by the Detectives, my cousin Joe Buyak called and I spoke with him for a few minutes. He wanted to make sure I was okay and asked me if I would like him at the Barracks for support. I told him that everything was fine and that the interview would take a couple of hours, so not to bother coming. Around 10:30 pm I finally sat down with two detectives from Troop E's Criminal Investigations Unit and gave them my statement about the shooting. I had been going over the shooting in my mind for four and a half hours since it happened. The preparation time helped me give the detectives a detailed summary. I wasn't worried about the interview or the pending Internal Affairs investigation because I had gone through the same process the first time around, and now at least, I knew what to expect. I also knew, like the first time around, I had nothing to hide.

During the interview Detective Norm Nault asked me why I smashed out the passenger side window of Parsons' car. While thinking about my response I began to laugh. I'd known Norm for a long time, so I didn't feel uncomfortable with my outburst. When he asked me what was so funny, I told him it was the first time in my six year career that I had been able to break a window! I recounted some of the unsuccessful attempts I'd had after a pursuit or a motor vehicle accident. We both laughed, and then I told him it was pure instinct. I was reacting to the information the desk troopers had provided to me; Parsons was intoxicated, armed, and ready to hurt any trooper who tried to stop him. I knew that whatever was going to happen had to happen right then and there. I had hoped to pull Parsons out of the car before he could do anything. It was my responsibility to keep Parsons from fleeing the scene by car or by foot. I didn't want to give him the opportunity to drive off and injure anyone with his car and I especially didn't want him to harm anyone inside of McDonalds. What I hadn't counted on was Parsons pulling out a loaded .38 revolver and pointing it at my head.

Norm said that smashing the window had been a good diversionary tactic that probably saved my life as well as Stowell's. I hadn't thought about it that way. What if I hadn't run up to the car and smashed out the window? Would things have turned out the same way? What if I had waited for Stowell to get Blizzard out of his cruiser and approach Parsons on the driver's side? Would Stowell have seen the gun? Would he have been shot? These questions kept running through my head for the rest of the interview.

The interview ended at about 12:30 am on Monday morning, December 28, 1998. Prior to leaving for the night I told Kenny Washburn, the union representative, that I couldn't and wouldn't work on the desk during the investigation. I would have a nervous breakdown if I was given that punishment again. Kenny said he would make sure the Department understood.

Stowell and I drove back to my parents' house although I can't remember if we drove together or separately. My father had picked up Wendy and Amelia and brought them to his house. My mother was waiting at the door, crying. Both my parents hugged me and my mother hugged Stowell. I hugged and kissed my wife and daughter, and then we all sat down and talked about the night. Over a few beers, Stowell and I explained to Wendy and my parents what we had been through.

When I reflected on the events of the night before falling asleep, I was glad that I had been involved in the first shooting because it mentally prepared me for the second one. My previous experience of dealing with an armed suspect allowed me to react more quickly and effectively in this incident. If I hadn't shot and killed somebody two years earlier, I may have hesitated in killing Joseph Parsons, which may have resulted in my death or the death of my friend Stowell, and possibly other deaths in that parking lot. I also knew what lay ahead in terms of the investigations. I'd been through all the bullshit before. What I didn't know was what lay ahead emotionally, and how hard I would fall from this fateful evening. But that night I went to bed and slept like a baby.

Chapter 7

Interview with Bonnie Patterson
by Deborah L. Mandel

"He truly is my hero"
Bonnie Patterson

"You never know what can happen," Bonnie Patterson, John's mother, said to me as we sat in a local pub for this interview. "As a parent you never stop being concerned about your children, even when they are adults and living their own lives."

This may be especially true for someone in Bonnie's position; the mother of two police officers. We had met to discuss her personal reactions to her son's involvement in the two fatal shootings, while on duty. I was also curious about her assessment, as his mother, of how John dealt in the aftermath of the incidents. Bonnie began by talking about some of the situations she had heard about from John regarding life as a police officer, each one traumatic.

"Some time ago," she began, "John stopped a travel van on Interstate 95 for what he thought would be a routine traffic violation and found one of the passengers carrying a gun and wearing a bullet-proof vest. Another time John got a call regarding an unruly crowd outside a bar in Groton. When he and his backup responded they were confronted with several hundred out of control patrons. A number of these patrons approached him in a threatening manner and he suffered a broken finger from that incident. Then a few years ago John helped remove the body of a child hidden in a tool box in the back of his father's truck. The child's head had been blown off with a shotgun by his father."

Leaning forward, a look of intensity on her face, she continued to recount, in a matter of fact manner, that when John first joined the force he came home and described a murder/suicide scene to his father, Gary, and her. He had responded to a call at a trailer park in 95 degree heat and when he entered the trailer there was blood dripping from the ceiling and the walls were covered in blood.

"I only know a minute amount of the stories," Bonnie said. "How could anyone not be affected by this?"

"John is currently out on medical leave because he was re-injured in the line of duty," she continued. He suffered a shoulder injury during the second shooting and recently during another work related scuffle, re-injured the shoulder and had to have surgery to repair it."

She talked calmly, telling me these tales, as I wondered about her inner emotional state. I asked her about the impact of hearing these stories. She replied that she was used to it. As the daughter of a police officer in Hartford, she grew up with police business as a part of her daily life.

"It was a different time," she said. "Police officers back then were respected and there wasn't the violence there is now. Today they are not respected at all. When I was growing up we didn't have as much fear of it being a dangerous job. There were other concerns, though. Because my sister, Maureen, and my younger brother, John, and I were the children of a cop, we weren't allowed to do a lot of the typical teenage stuff. We couldn't go to football games or baseball games. If we did we'd be presumed to be trollops or street walkers, not fine young ladies, as the daughters of a well-respected police officer should be. Then one day, after 27 years on the force, my father was beat up by a man who had just been brought into the police station and broken free of the arresting officers. That was the day he decided to leave the force and retire."

Police work is a family affair with Bonnie's relatives. Besides her father, Bonnie's brother is a retired Hartford Police Captain and now a Federal Marshal. This brother's second wife, now deceased, was the first woman Sergeant in the Hartford Police. Bonnie's daughter is a detective in Fairfax County, VA, one nephew is a Lieutenant, another a Captain in the Hartford force and a niece is a retired Hartford Police Detective. Gary's father, John's grandfather, was also a detective in the Hartford Force. When John applied to the Connecticut State Police in his sophomore year of college in 1990, it came as no surprise. Her brother, John's uncle, whom he and his siblings and cousins worshiped as children, was the catalyst for John wanting to join the force. When John's cousins Joe and Laura became officers, John wanted to follow in all of their footsteps.

Because of funding issues in the state, new troopers were not hired for several years. When the hiring freeze ended, there were thousands of applicants for only a few positions. Out of 8,000 applicants, John was chosen as one of the 80 recruits in July 1992. He was six credits short of graduating from the University of Connecticut when he was accepted into the Academy. Bonnie made him promise to finish school, but supported his decision to join at that time. He eventually graduated with a degree in Sociology.

I asked Bonnie about her memories of the first shooting incident. It was a warm evening on September 3rd, 1996. Bonnie and Gary were at home watching TV, the front door open to let in the evening air. Bonnie, who was already in her pajamas, noticed a flashlight shining into their front living room window, and heard a knock on the open front door. She recognized the officer, who said he had to speak to both of them. Initially, Bonnie thought nothing of it; she had no premonition of John being in any trouble, perhaps due to a lifetime spent around the police.

"After inviting him in, he told us John and his fellow officer, Jay Gaughan, had been involved in a shooting. John and Jay were uninjured, but another man was dead. We were stunned. Upon hearing John was involved in a shooting, I went into instant shock."

A short time later another Trooper arrived to be with the couple. Neither officer had much information to share with John's parents, only that John was being brought back to the barracks and that they could not contact him.

"I remember sitting there in disbelief—almost unable to move. There was a continuing conversation, but I remember none of what was discussed," Bonnie said. "Thankfully John called shortly thereafter and told us he was okay. Then he started talking about a doctor's appointment that he had the next day."

"Should I keep it?" John asked her. Bonnie figured he was shutting down by focusing on such a trivial detail. But his conversation kept going back to that appointment.

"I think he was desperately trying to focus his thoughts away from the shooting," Bonnie said.

"We'll figure that out tomorrow. Just deal with what you have to do tonight. Is there anything you want me to do for you right now?"

John asked her to inform his sisters and his cousin Joe Buyak, who at the time was a Lieutenant on the Hartford Police Force and ask Joe to come to the Montville barracks to be with him. John figured that while the department would not let his parents come, they might allow Joe in because he was an officer. Bonnie immediately called her two older daughters, Tracy and Maureen. John's younger sister, Christine, who was only 13 at the time was already in her room asleep. Next Bonnie called her nephew. Joe's wife answered the phone and wanted to chit-chat. Bonnie was desperate to talk to Joe and tell him about John's plight. Finally she got through to her that she needed to talk to Joe. When he got on the phone, Bonnie told him what had happened.

"I'm on my way," Joe said. Bonnie figures Joe probably went in his pajamas. The troop did let him stay with John for the night, and accompany him to the site during the reenactment. Bonnie was relieved that Joe could be there, given that she and Gary couldn't. When the investigation was over, Joe brought John home, where they were joined by another cousin, also named John.

"I don't remember what we did about the doctor's appointment," Bonnie said.

Bonnie already had experienced the devastating impact that killing in the line of duty can bring. Her sister-in-law Barbara Moriarty Bowen had been involved in a justified shooting while a Sergeant in the Hartford Police Department. Barbara's account of the follow-up to the shooting was brief and to the point. When she returned to headquarters her debriefing consisted of three sentences.

"You okay?"

"I'm okay."

"Okay then."

That was it. She did not ask for, nor was she offered any counseling. Bonnie speculated that Barbara kept all her feelings to herself after her shooting incident. A few years later, in her late thirties, she developed breast cancer. The two crises were overwhelming and she shut everyone out of her life. There was a period of time when Bonnie and her sister did not see Barbara or talk to her. She would not talk to anyone. Bonnie tried, unsuccessfully, to keep in touch with her.

"We all felt helpless," Bonnie said. "I believe she was showing all the signs of someone very troubled. We tried to get my brother John to intervene, but she did a pretty good job of not letting him know what was going on with her health and would never talk to a professional about what she was going through. I think she felt if she didn't talk to anyone about her cancer and the shooting it would all go away."

When Barbara became sick enough to need help, she allowed Bonnie and Maureen back in her life. They alternately cared for her.

"During the unbearably long journey to her death, she finally opened up about her thoughts," Bonnie said. "She knew she was dying, and she was devastated by the knowledge that she had killed someone. She was guilt-ridden and she believed that she would be punished by God for eternity. God would not forgive her for taking the life of another human being. Heaven would not be waiting for her; she was convinced she'd go to Hell for killing someone. It bothered her until she died, at age forty-three."

Bonnie hopes they had convinced her that God did not have to forgive her for anything and that she would indeed spend eternity in Heaven.

"I felt that she had begun to accept that she had no choice in the shooting and was doing her job. She did, after all, save the lives of her fellow officers as well as other civilians—she did the job she was expected to do."

John, sixteen at the time of his aunt's death, was a pall bearer. He had no idea that in a few years he would be facing those same demons.

The second shooting happened on a Sunday night, December 27, 1998. Bonnie remembers the day, because her daughter and son-in-law, Maureen and Michael, had just left to go back to Virginia after spending Christmas with the family. Bonnie and Gary spent the day house cleaning.

During the afternoon Gary went out to the grocery store and when he returned he told Bonnie that he had heard on the car radio that there had been a shooting in Lisbon involving a gunman and the police. He said a prayer that the shooting did not involve John. They knew nothing else until later in the evening when John called. Bonnie answered the phone but John asked to speak to his father, she knows now, to protect her. At the time she suspected that something was wrong. She heard only Gary's side of the conversation.

"Okay."

"Okay."

"You okay?"

Three sentences eerily similar to her sister-in-law's debriefing. Then she heard Gary ask John if they could come to the barracks. The answer was no. Gary filled her in on what had happened. John asked his parents to call Wendy, his sisters and his cousins. Bonnie first called his sisters and then called her sister Maureen in Sprague to tell her, distressed by this recent turn of events. They were still celebrating the holiday, because her niece and nephews were all at her sister's house. The three cousins, all of whom were police officers, immediately left for the barracks, but this time the department allowed no one to be with John.

Next Bonnie called her brother John. She vividly remembers her brother's response to her concern about John's involvement in a second shooting.

"He was doing his job, don't even think anything else," he said. Those words rang true to her. John was doing his job. Yet he was her son, once again in a life and death situation.

Bonnie had a difficult time contacting Wendy, as she was still in Rhode Island visiting her family, and her cell phone was turned off. A short while later a Police Officer came to their home to talk to them about the shooting. Some of the evening is a blur to her, she believes as a result of being in shock.

"So much of what happened during the time of both shootings is difficult to remember—probably because it was such a difficult time for John," Bonnie said.

The shock and disorientation that Bonnie describes can be related to the phenomenon called "vicarious traumatization" or "secondary trauma". Facing the fact that her son was in not only one, but two, shootings, brought on a shock reaction. Family members might also experience difficulty sleeping, nightmares, avoidance, depression, or loss of interest in things previously important to them. As seen with Barbara, Bonnie's sister-in-law, officers themselves are not getting the help they need, and the families, who also need support during these times, are even less likely to have their concerns addressed.

Because John was married at the time of the second shooting, he did not come home to Bonnie and Gary, so she was not as aware of his reactions as she had been the first time. She was, however, still extremely concerned and worried.

"Sometime after the second episode, I read a newspaper story about John and I was horrified to find out how completely devastated he was by the shooting," said Bonnie. John had, according to the article, broken down at the site of the incident in the arms of his Sergeant, unable to fathom that this could happen again. Bonnie was heartbroken that he had been so affected by this second shooting, knowing how troubled he still was by the first incident.

It fell on Wendy's shoulders to deal with everything John was going through. Bonnie would call Wendy often to make sure he was okay and getting the help he needed, but didn't always hear the answer she hoped for. Knowing that John would not want to upset her, Bonnie would often ask her husband to call John to see how he was doing. John's response was always the same, he was doing okay. Everything was not okay, though. After the second shooting, and in conjunction with Wendy's pregnancy with their youngest son, Wendy and John were having significant marital difficulties.

Bonnie and Gary were not privy to most of what was going on, until one day Wendy called to say she was sending John 'home' to his parents. John came to talk to them. John told his parents that Wendy accused him of being emotionless, of not being able to share his feelings. John denied it. Bonnie asked him when the last time he had cried was.

"When you were diagnosed with cancer," he told his mom, and immediately burst into tears.

This broke the dam he had erected around his feelings, and he was able to go home to Wendy in a more open state. Once John began to acknowledge these pent up feelings, they were able to work on re-establishing their relationship.

John had done the best he could to put the first shooting in perspective. His friends were a big support, rallying around him. He and Wendy, who were engaged at the time, focused on planning their wedding, looking forward to purchasing a house, and traveling. He also started boxing, which became a passion.

After the second shooting, Bonnie noticed that John became even more compulsive about keeping busy. He had to plan more vacations, he had to take more trips, he had to move, and he had to build a new house. She believes that he felt if he worked at something difficult enough he could forget what happened. John had always been a passionate person; in love with life, his family, his career. He was a funny guy, keeping his sisters, nieces and nephews laughing. He had always been attentive to her and Gary. But after the shootings even his passion became more compulsive. He became more attentive, more worried, more involved.

One way that John expended energy was by training to box in the Police Olympics. Bonnie and Gary, along with Wendy, baby Amelia, and John's sister Christine traveled to Stockholm, Sweden (the birth-place of John's great grandparents) in 1999, to watch him compete in his first Olympics. John's decision to box in the Police Olympics had been worrisome, but not surprising.

"I was concerned that he would get seriously injured, but he loves to participate in sports at all levels, so it became exciting for us. Plus it gave John another outlet to channel his focus away from his worries." Four years later, in 2003, they traveled with Wendy, Amelia, his son Eric, and his sisters Maureen and Christine to Barcelona, Spain. They had an amazing time during both trips, despite the difficulty Bonnie had in watching the actual matches, providing John with a very loud and happy cheering section. He did not win a gold medal in either Olympics, but, according to her, he did his barracks proud.

John remains very attentive to his parents' needs, frequently calling and visiting. Once, a few years ago, calling his mother, he heard unusual noises in the background. He demanded to know where they were. His father, who had been dealing with some heart issues, had not been feeling well, and Bonnie had taken him to the emergency room. John, hearing this, immediately rushed to be with them in the hospital. He is attuned to what is going on in the family and wants to be there and help whenever he can.

According to Bonnie, he was always this way. When John was two, he and his sister Tracy had to stay at their grandparents' home for an extended period of time while their three year old sister Maureen was in the hospital. When she returned to pick them up, after ten days, she was told that John had not let go of Tracy's hand the whole time.

Bonnie continues to worry about her only son, but realizes she has no control over what happens in his life. She thinks that the shootings have affected John more than he lets on. He still doesn't talk much about the incidents but she accepts that he is an adult and does not want to tell his parents everything. She was concerned when he became depressed and anxious following the shootings. He finally agreed to start therapy after experiencing a bout of recurring nightmares where he was stab-bing someone over and over again and when he saw the face of the victim it was the face of his Dad. This prompted him to call for help.

Bonnie is relieved that John likes his therapist and has found the process helpful. She is grateful that he has more opportunities than her sister-in-law Barbara had when she faced the same issues. But John had to fight to get this help. When he first started therapy, the state only provided six counseling sessions. His parents volunteered to pay for any out of pocket expenses John would incur if he continued on his own. Knowing that what he was dealing with would take more than six sessions, John filed an objection to the number of sessions which prompted the Governor to form a commission to study the situation. Unbeknownst to his family, John testified at a hearing to determine what services should be available. It was an emotional experience. John cried on the stand, expressing his opinion that unlimited sessions were absolutely necessary. The commission voted in favor of John's request, and police officers now have been granted unlimited sessions. John's sister Tracy found out about the hearing through a friend who worked at the TV station that John had just testified before the commission, and that it was going to be televised.

"Your brother did you proud," her friend told her. "He is probably the reason the commission voted in favor of the change."

Adding to the trauma of the shootings, after the second incident, John was sued by the father of the victim. John kept his court appearance very low key. "I don't think he wanted us to worry that it was a big deal, even though it was so huge," Bonnie said. "I think because the shooting had already been found justifiable by the department, he was confident that he would be found innocent of all charges. But he did not realize how emotional the entire process would be."

When his trial came up, John did not want his mother to go to court with him. He expressed concern that having her there would be too emotional for him, and if he looked at her he would cry. This indicated to Bonnie that there was more going on beneath the surface than John let on to. Wendy attended court to support John, which was comforting, but not overwhelming. He was found not guilty.

Despite the intensity of the situation, John expressed concern for the dead man's father, who he believed did not know much about what kind of person his son was. He had empathy for the man who had sued him, empathy for the father who found out over the course of the trial what his son was like, who lost his case and then had to pay all of John's legal fees. This is typical behavior for John; passion and empathy for others. It is what keeps him going in his job and in his life.

Bonnie believes that the shootings still bother John and that he suffers, for some of the same reasons as her sister-in-law. "Because of the love he was raised with, taking a life was no small matter, even though it was justified."

She is also aware of the danger he continues to face every day. When her daughter Maureen was about to enter the recruiting class to become a Fairfax County, Virginia police officer, Bonnie's son-in-law, Maureen's husband, asked John how often he drew his gun. His answer both shocked and frightened her. He told Michael he drew his gun every day.

"He truly is my hero," Bonnie said. "How many parents can make that claim? When I think of all that John has been through, I am so proud of him for, at least on the surface, being so upbeat and funny. I know it is a struggle for him every day to overcome what he has had to deal with. John is a wonderful husband, incredible father, loving and caring son and brother and HERO to us all. We love him dearly. In my mind, for all he has been through, he can do anything he wants. From a mother's perspective, he did not get the recognition he deserved."

Bonnie hopes that writing about his experience is healing for John. Through this process, she anticipates that he will let go of the angst he carries inside. She prays that he will find the peace he needs to justify to himself that he was doing his job. In some ways, the first shooting, she believes, was more difficult for John because he feels that there were other options. John watched the man kiss his dogs good-bye, crying as he did so. Then came the demands that they better kill him before he killed them, as he ran toward them with a knife in his hand. These events led John to consider that it was a set up for a suicide-by-cop. The second shooting happened when the perpetrator had a gun pointed at John's head. This one she feels he is more at peace with because there clearly was no other choice.

Bonnie knows that given the circumstances of two shootings, John could be a complete emotional wreck. She is grateful that he has been proactive and chosen to get help for himself, something that many police officers cannot or will not do. He has chosen to pursue counseling. She knows the struggles her sister-in-law had and hopes that John can be spared the same intense distress. The bottom line for Bonnie is simple. "I am proud of John for all that he has accomplished both in and out of the line of duty."

Chapter 8

Déjà vu

The morning following Parsons' shooting was an exact duplicate of the morning after the first shooting. It reminded me of the movie Ground Hog Day when Bill Murray kept waking up to a replay of the same day, over and over and over again. I received phone calls from friends, family and coworkers who wanted to know how my family and I were doing. It was refreshing to realize I had such widespread support. Troopers from other barracks throughout the state, who I didn't even know, called to wish me the best. But once again the leadership of the Connecticut State Police failed me. Not one person from the Command Staff called, causing my hatred for the department to deepen.

And again, they did not support me in the media. The news articles all referenced my first shooting in Jewett City and reported that my current actions would be investigated within the department. Not once did the department support my actions while I was being ridiculed by the press. All they needed to say was that my actions were justified based upon the preliminary information they had and that the incident was under investigation. But no one in senior management had the balls or decency to say that or stand up for my rights.

I had a good laugh though when my friend Jeff Ross called me at home that morning, and told me how cool it was to be friends with a serial killer. When I heard those words, I said, Holy shit, you're right. I am a serial killer! We both laughed about it and talked about what had happened. Jeff said that when he heard about the shooting on the news, he knew that it had to be me because I was the only officer with enough balls to shoot someone again. He laughed doubly hard when I told him I'd shot off this guy's pinky, just like in the first shooting, and that Mr. Waffles at work was calling me "pinky killer".

I don't want anyone to think that I'm a cold-hearted person because of my reaction to Jeff's statement. What most people don't realize is that most police officers make jokes to deal with traumatic events. It's standard operating procedure. It's what keeps us sane. You can't deal with this high level of stress day in and day out without having a release valve. Not that shooting someone is funny, but laughing at it with Jeff was a defense mechanism to let off some of the tension. When I joked about the shooting it seemed less real. I had developed this macabre sense of humor to deal with the ungodly, gruesome things I'd been exposed to over the course of my career. I'd had to learn this coping skill early on in my career.

The first of many critical incidents happened before I was officially hired as a state trooper and was still a student at The University of Connecticut. One Saturday morning I was traveling down I-95 in New London, headed to work as a banquet waiter in Mystic. It was in the middle of a snowstorm, and the roads were icy. Suddenly, a car lost control in front of me, as it entered the highway from the on ramp. In slow motion I watched as it shot straight across the highway and slammed head-on into the side of a tractor trailer. The operator of the car was thrown through his driver's side window, landing face down on the snow covered road. He slid headlong into a bridge abutment. I was able to safely slow down and pull my car over to the side of the road. I ran up to the man. He appeared to be in his mid-sixties, and much to my astonishment, he was up on all fours, facing away from me. There was a mound of blood covered snow beneath his head and I could see that blood was still dripping from somewhere. When I asked him if he was okay, he turned and looked at me, a look of horror on his face, his eyes begging me for help. It was then that I noticed the gaping hole in the center of his forehead. It looked as if someone had taken an ice cream scoop and dug out the skin and muscles from his forehead. I could see bone. It reminded me of the scene in Stephen King's movie, Pet Sematary when Dr. Louis Creed was treating accident victim Victor Pazcow's head injury. It was that gross.

With the assistance of the truck driver, I was able to lay the injured man on the ground. I took off my shirt and covered the wound on his forehead and the truck driver got a blanket from his vehicle. We took care of the man as best we could until the State Police and an ambulance arrived. Throughout the day at work I thought about what I had seen, and even though I was glad to have stopped and helped the victim, it made me sad to think about it. This was the first time in my life I had seen someone badly injured. Helping him, despite the goriness of his injury, reinforced my determination to become a police officer. I went to visit him in the hospital that night, after my shift was over. I thought about him frequently in the weeks to come, but gradually, like most memories, it faded some. However it left a mark, like a tattoo on my heart.

The second incident occurred shortly after graduating from the State Police Academy in January of 1993. I was dispatched to assist EMS with a medical call in Montville, with my field training officer Bill Flanagan. En route to the scene we were advised that a young boy had been hit by a falling tree in the middle of the woods. When we arrived, the boy's friends brought us to the injured youth, who was already being treated by the EMS, and filled us in on what had happened. While playing in the woods the group had decided to try and push over a large, dead tree. As the tree began to fall, the boys scattered, running in different directions, but the tree hit that one boy. His body had been crushed and mangled by the force of the huge old tree falling on him. The boys ranged in age from ten to twelve years, and they looked scared beyond belief as they watched the EMS personnel trying to keep their friend alive. As they worked on him, he started to throw up nasty, green colored mucus. When they were ready to transport him, Bill and I assisted in carrying the injured boy out of the woods, as he continued to throw up the green, slime-like mucus. Sadly, the child died a week later from the injuries he had sustained. It has been over twenty years since that day and I can still picture the boy's face and that green slime. Even though in the intervening years I have witnessed even more gruesome events, I still vividly remember that scene. This is most likely due to the fact that it involved a child. For me, this is the most difficult situation of all. To this day, I will not look at an autopsy of a child. No one may notice, but I always turn the other way.

The third episode in my personal log of life's most gruesome days occurred a few years after I became a trooper. I was dispatched to a trailer park in Griswold to check on the well-being of a woman who hadn't been heard from in a few days. The woman lived in the trailer with her boyfriend. Her ex-husband had made the call, as he was concerned about her. When I arrived on scene I noticed the woman's vehicle was parked next to the trailer. It was a blue Honda civic. I knocked on the trailer door; no response. When I asked the neighbors if they had seen the woman recently, they said that they hadn't seen either the man or the woman in several days. After advising the troop about the information the neighbors provided me, I asked over the air if I could force entry into the trailer. I was advised that Sergeant Wakely was en-route to assist me. When he arrived, Wakely broke a small window adjacent to the front door and looked into the trailer. He turned to me and whispered that there was a man lying on the floor of the trailer and that there was blood everywhere. The Sergeant reached in through the broken window and opened the front door. We entered with our guns drawn, and I observed a man lying on the floor, in front of a chair, with a rifle lying next to him. He had obviously put the barrel of the rifle in his mouth and blown off the back of his head. There was blood splattered on the wall behind the chair and on the ceiling, and it looked as if someone had shot a couple of red paintballs in the corner where the ceiling and wall came together.

Not knowing the intricacies of a murder-suicide, and still a rookie, I believed the woman might still be alive. How naïve I was! As I tactically peered around the door jam to the bedroom at the end of the hall, I could see the woman's feet at the bottom of the bed. When I entered the bedroom, I observed the woman was lying on her back on the bed with fifty or sixty stab wounds to her neck, breasts, torso and vaginal area. It looked fake. There wasn't a lot of blood and she was simply lying there with her eyes open. Even though it must have been a horrible death—suffocating because her lungs had been punctured and drowning in her own blood—it was eerily peaceful. I think that's why it affected me so much. I apologize ahead of time for my inhumane and sadistic humor—but I did notice that she had nice tits. That's what I'm talking about—humor relieves stress. I learned early on not to take anything to heart: to make fun of shitty situations including things like this. It's a perverted defense mechanism that has only worsened with time.

There were uncountable incidents during my career. In the mid 1990's my father told me that there had just been a report on the news of police being shot at down the road from our house. I got in my cruiser and rushed to the scene. When I arrived, I learned that responding officers had been fired upon after knocking on the door of an apartment while conducting a well-being search. After the SWAT team entered and cleared the apartment, investigating officers were able to determine what had transpired. At the exact moment the officers were knocking on the door, an elderly male shot his sister with a 7.62 German rifle. Thinking that they were being fired upon, the officers cleared out of the building and advised the troop as such. After killing his sister, the elderly male sat on his bed, put the rifle in his mouth, pulled the trigger and blew half his head off. The force of the bullet entering and exiting his head caused him to fall over and lie down on the side of the bed. Sadly, the poor bastard hadn't killed himself. So the tough old guy sat up, placed the barrel of the rifle in front of the remaining side of his face and pulled the trigger again, removing all doubt of death this time.

Once investigators completed their investigation, and prior to the medical examiner's office removing both bodies, I was given the grand tour of the crime scene. It was gruesome. There was blood all over the bedroom where the man had killed himself. There were brains all over the bed, wall and floor, and pieces of skull everywhere. Most of all, I'll never forget the single eye lying on the floor underneath the bedside table. One eye! I didn't know if it was the left or right. Didn't matter, I guess. It was fucked up either way.

One summer afternoon I was working a Highway Construction Project—an overtime job—when I heard troopers being dispatched to an accident with injuries only a few miles away. After learning that both troopers were already handling other investigations, I advised the troop that I would respond. En route to the accident I was told that the operator had been partially ejected and was pinned under the vehicle.

Great, I thought. More blood and guts. Accident injuries are perverse because they usually encompass all body parts and are grotesque at best. This would be no different. When I arrived on the scene I saw the vehicle lying on its side, passenger door to the sky. The undercarriage of the vehicle was facing me. Five people were standing on the other side of the car pointing towards the ground. One woman had her hand over her mouth in disbelief. As I retrieved my first aid kit and ran towards them, I prayed that the ambulance would get there quickly.

In the academy we're trained to be Medical Response Technicians (MRTs), but our training is mostly a joke. I tell people that if you're having a heart attack, choking or having trouble breathing, we're your men. Other than that, you can kiss your ass goodbye. I know it seems like a contradiction, but the general public believes we are all mighty, when in reality we are not able to treat their injuries. Most people we just comfort and tell them "the ambulance is on its way."

As I walked around the front of the vehicle I saw the operator lying partially out of the driver's window, with his spine bent backwards at a perfect 90 degree angle. He was flailing his arms around as if he were trying to crawl out of the vehicle and get himself free, all the while spitting out blood bubbles and gasping for air. I felt bad for the guy, like, "damn, that sucks." It was pretty fucked up. I had never seen anything like it before and never have since.

What made it worse was the group of people staring at me and wondering what I was going to do. The shitty thing was that there was nothing I could do. I thought about driving my cruiser over and pushing the operator's car onto my cruiser and pulling him out, but I could tell that he would be dead soon and that it wouldn't help.

So the only logical thing to do was watch him die. One hundred and fifty years ago I would have shot him in the head so he wouldn't have to suffer. Today that wasn't an option. After explaining the situation to the observers, I asked them to return to their vehicles. Although they were all upset about what was happening, deep down they understood my moral dilemma.

I knelt down next to the dying man and flat out told him that he was going to die and that he needed to stop trying to move so he wouldn't prolong his suffering. The sad thing was that he took my advice; he stopped flailing around, the adrenaline drained from his body and he died a moment later.

As hard as it was to see this man in such agony, that wasn't the part of the incident that upset and traumatized me. The worst part occurred when the day shift supervisor arrived. Once he learned of the operator's demise he told me that we had to "get him outta here." Not that he was stating the obvious or anything. So he asked me how I thought we should do it. My idea was that once the wrecker operator arrived, he could tie onto the undercarriage of the vehicle and slowly lift it off his body so that we could pull him out and get him into the meat wagon. Great idea, right? Nope. The sergeant went with his plan, but at least he asked me first.

So here's the scenario. As I was engaged in a conversation with my sergeant, EMS and fire personnel were walking around the scene waiting for us to make our decision and the people that I had shagged away from the accident were still waiting in their cars. Our conversation went something like this:

HIM: "Okay kid, I want you and the wrecker operator to push the vehicle over so we can get him out of the car."

ME: "Won't he bounce around in the car when we do it."

HIM: "So."

ME: "Don't you think when he's bouncing around like a pinball there will be blood flying all over the place."

HIM: "So."

ME: "I really don't care how we get him out of the car but I think everyone else will have a problem with it."

HIM: "Just do it."

ME: "Okay." I answered with a sarcastic smile, as if to say you're a fucking retard.

As you can imagine, he did bounce around like a pinball, blood did go everywhere and everyone on scene witnessed the entire show and was mortified by it. Just another day on the Connecticut State Police.

Chapter 9

Forgive me Father for I have sinned

On December 29th, about forty-eight hours after the Parsons shooting, I went out with Wendy, Stowell, Kerry, and Jay to a local bar for a few drinks to discuss the shooting. We sat around and each shared our version of what happened. It was validating to me that what I had heard and seen was the same as what Stowell and Kerry experienced. After a few hours of intense conversation, I went home and like the previous night, slept soundly.

During the shooting, I had hit and injured my shoulder on the passenger side door jamb of the car as I was ducking for cover. When I went to the doctor, he told me I might have torn a ligament or two and would need four to six weeks of physical therapy. That was a huge relief. It enabled me to stay home and spend lots of time with my newborn daughter, Amelia Hope, who was born at the end of November and had just celebrated her first Christmas. Having the time off would allow me to help my wife care for her, which I hoped would distract me from thinking about what had happened. I sure as hell wasn't going to sit on the desk like I had after the first shooting and get depressed. During my recovery I was able to somewhat distance myself from the Connecticut State Police and my duties as a Connecticut State Trooper, and in retrospect, I realize that taking that time off helped me psychologically by giving me space to process both shootings and to start the healing process.

A few days after the incident I received a telephone call from my sister Maureen who was attending the Fairfax County, Virginia Police Academy. After we talked about what had happened to me, I asked her to reconsider her career choice. It made me sick to think about her having to survive in our fucked up society. I didn't want her to see the things I had seen and I definitely didn't want her to do the ungodly and sinful things that I had done. I didn't quite beg her to quit, but I strongly encouraged her to leave the academy and choose a safer career. I even asked my brother-in-law, her husband, to talk to her about it. However, Maureen was adamant about finishing the academy and becoming a police officer, so even though I disagreed with her decision, I supported her.

Maureen and I had been raised Catholic and were taught at an early age that taking the life of another human being was the biggest of all sins. I was an altar boy and attended church services faithfully in my youth. I was brought up to believe in the importance of religion and to respect the Catholic Church and all it had to offer. When I became an adult, however, it didn't take me long to figure out that the Catholic Church is a hypocritical bureaucracy and one of the biggest money making businesses in the world. I came to believe that the church did not care about its followers, because if it did, they wouldn't protect the pedophile priests who victimized thousands of children. The last time I went to church (except for a wedding or funeral—oops, same thing) the priest, during his sermon, asked the members of the congregation to give an extra donation for the attorney fees incurred by a priest who was arrested for molesting children. I told my father that would be the last time I would ever enter a church. But it was not the last time I thought about God.

After the shootings, thoughts about what I had done in the eyes of God began to creep into my mind. Looking at it His way, I was a sinner. While I thought I was able to recognize the difference between killing and murdering a person, it really wasn't that simple. On the one hand, the killings of Joseph Cote and Joseph Parsons were a necessary evil in order to protect myself, Jay, the neighborhood kids, and Stowell. But was it still a sin in the eyes of God? Morally, part of me believed it was the right thing to do under the circumstances of those nights. But on the other hand it presented me with a dilemma—I had chosen a profession that was honorable, but went against everything I was brought up to believe.

After the second shooting, my parents suggested more than once that I attend church again. They believed it might help me process the mental trauma I was dealing with. While there was some appeal to that, I questioned how I would walk into church, sit down in a confessional and say to a priest; forgive me Father for I have sinned. It's been ten years since my last confession and, oh by the way, I've killed two people. I'd be saying Hail Marys for a year.

This was part of why I didn't want Maureen to become a police woman. I never wanted her to face this mortal sin. But another part of me didn't want her to become a cop because she was a woman, even though over the years, my long-held belief that women shouldn't become cops had changed dramatically. Early in my career I firmly believed that women weren't physically capable of handling themselves in most situations that police officers become involved in. If I were getting my ass kicked by a three hundred pound guy cracked out of his mind, would I want a male police officer responding to the call or a female officer? That seemed like a no-brainer. But some of the women I've assisted on the job have helped me to realize that having the heart and the willingness to get involved in dangerous situations counts for a lot and gets things done. While this has softened my stance on the issue, and even though the Connecticut State Police is full of pussies—male police officers who are afraid of their own shadows—I would still want a male police officer helping me. No offense, ladies.

During the second week of February, my family and I went to Virginia for Maureen's graduation from the Academy. I tried talking with her again about her career choice, detailing the impending dangers that come with the job. We talked more about what happened to me and how different the second shooting was from my first deadly encounter. I tried to explain to her how dangerous the world really was and how she needed to accept and understand that early on in her career. While I was extremely proud of Maureen for completing the academy and had every intention of supporting her, I was terrified about her safety. Her police agency patrolled the towns, cities and highways in and around the Washington DC area, one of the most dangerous cities in the United States. I prayed that she never had to do the things that I had done or see the things that I had seen in my short, six-year career.

The only advice I ended up giving Maureen that day was for her to shoot first and answer questions later. She was a woman, I said, and if she felt like someone was getting the upper hand on her in a fight, shoot them!! In our society women are considered to be weaker than men and I told her the Criminal Courts were aware of this and she would be able to use this defense to her advantage, if need be. My sister looks like a Barbie doll. She is six feet tall, with blond hair and blue eyes and probably weighs 130 pounds. If she were getting her ass kicked by a 250 pound man and thought that she was going to black out, I wanted her to kill him. I needed her to believe she had enough intestinal fortitude to make the ultimate, split second decision to take another person's life in order to save her own. I wanted her to understand that in police work it was survival of the fittest. She needed to prepare herself for battle, I told her, to insure her ultimate survival as a Fairfax County Police Officer.

At the close of the ceremony I had the honor of pinning my sister's badge on her new uniform.

Before the ceremony Maureen had warned me that her instructors and fellow police recruits were aware that I had recently been involved in my second deadly shooting and they wanted to meet me after the ceremony. I wasn't sure how that would go. But when she introduced me to them, they all gave me words of encouragement. None of them asked me about what happened, and I was relieved that I didn't have to go into details about what I had gone through. Instead I could be the proud brother of the new rookie on the force, putting away all of my worries for the moment.

Chapter 10

I began having nightmares

A few days after pinning my sister's badge on her, I started working in the Criminal Investigation Unit (CIU). It was an easy transition because I had previously worked with all of the guys in the office, including the Detective Sergeant in charge. During the first couple of weeks I was given menial jobs, such as placing all of the mug-shot photos in new three-ring binders and preparing investigative paperwork packets for various crimes. Slowly, over the next few weeks, my sergeant allowed me to investigate crimes and assist other detectives in the office with their investigations.

One case that I asked to be assigned to involved a fourteen year old girl, April Dawn Pennington, who had been missing since May of 1996. I believed that she had been killed by a local pedophile, George Leniart, and I wanted to put the bastard in jail. With the assistance of Sergeant Rich and other detectives in the office, I re-investigated and re-interviewed most everyone who was involved in the case. I gave a polygraph to the main witness, PJ, who had been with Leniart and April before she disappeared. He admitted that Leniart had told him he would kill April before they even picked her up. During this investigation, thoughts of April were never far from my mind. I constantly went over her disappearance and probable death. While the investigation worked as a distraction it also added to the weight of my depression. This was the first time that I took work home with me. When I left the CIU a few years later, and went back on the road, I kept abreast of the case and passed on the sleepless nights to the guys who took the case over. It affected everyone.

Leniart had been arrested a few times by the mid-1990s. He had a history of hanging out with younger kids and he was out on bond after an arrest for sexually abusing and attempted strangling of a fourteen year old girl when April Pennington went missing. I knew about the case at the time, but was not directly involved in it. I knew he did it—call it cop's intuition if you want—but after five years on the force I'd learned about human nature and the propensity for repeat offenses by individuals like this guy. Leniart did his five years for the first conviction, and when he got out we rearrested him for breaking his probation when we found him running in the woods with a 14 year old Russian girl.

Many detectives worked long hours on this case. I once drove around for hours with an ex-girlfriend of Leniart's, hoping she would lead me to where he had dumped the body. Nothing came of that, or any of the other attempted ploys, like when one detective went bass fishing near Leniart and struck up a conversation. He carried a dozen eels in a bucket, a tape recorder in one pocket and a .38 revolver in the other. It was a good try, but all he got was Leniart placing the blame for April's disappearance on someone else.

We all knew better. Based on statements Leniart made to other prisoners while in jail, the State's Attorney put out a warrant for his arrest. What was unusual about this was that the body of the victim had not been recovered. When Leniart was finally arrested for the homicide of April Dawn Pennington on April 1, 2008, and charged with capital felony murder, my mind was eased a little, but I still thought about her all the time. I couldn't watch the trial because I was sequestered as a potential witness, but I did hear the closing argument. When the verdict came down, there were big smiles in the ranks; guilty of murder and three counts of capital felony; life imprisonment with no chance of parole. We celebrated, but to this day, April Dawn Pennington has not been found.

In appreciation for the relentless work we had done, eight of us from the State Police and the State's Attorney's Office were honored in a ceremony at the State Police Academy for bringing Leniart to justice against long odds.

Because of my work in Jewett City with sexual assault investigations, within a short time of working for Troop E's CIU, I became a sexual assault investigator. I handled cases involving the rape of infants, children, adults (both men and women), and Special Education Students. I also handled assaults, robberies and other crimes against persons. I honestly thought that by working in the CIU I would be able to clear my mind of all the bad shit I had seen and done over the years. I was going in to clean up a mess, not be the first responder. But only so many children had to explain to me how their grandfather, mother, father, brother, sister, babysitter, or neighbor finger-bombed (digitally penetrated) or sodomized them, before I started getting affected by it.

Once again it created a hate and total disconnect for humanity in my mind and I began to question my own being. As a trooper I spent long hours alone in my squad car, giving me lots of down time and ample opportunity to think. I began to question why we were here on this earth when so much of what I saw was one person hurting another person. I began to hate people with every breath I took. I thought that with all my years of experience dealing with heinous acts of violence I would have become numb, or learned to create a better barrier to keep me sane. But these stories were so sad, and tragically, avoidable. If the parents or guardians even cared a little bit for their children or loved ones, these abuses would never happen. But that's what I think is wrong with our society. People just don't care enough.

During my first month back to work after the second shooting I began having nightmares. They were all identical in theme. At some point during the dream I would be forced into saving somebody from someone with either a gun or a knife, and I would be unable to save them. Ninety-nine percent of the time my gun wouldn't fire, or if it did, the bullets would fall to the ground and miss their target. Sometimes water would come out of the gun and the asshole I was trying to kill would be covered with water, taunting me and laughing. In the beginning, a lot of these dreams had my father in them. The explanation I had for dreaming about my father was that he had always been there to protect me when I was growing up. In a way, maybe he was trying to protect me in these dreams, but I could never protect him. This saddened me and definitely exacerbated the problems I was starting to have with depression. I felt extreme helplessness in these dreams, so intense at times, that I would wake up in a cold sweat with my wife frantically asking me if I was okay. These dreams occurred two to three times a month.

I also began to experience momentary bouts of sadness and crying, generally when I was alone; driving, watching television, or lying in bed. I especially remember the Folger's Coffee commercial where the son comes home for Christmas to surprise his mother and little brother. Every time I saw it, I would bawl my eyes out. I'd go from lying quietly in bed to crying uncontrollably for no apparent reason. It always baffled me when it was happening and I never understood it. Looking back, it was apparent that depression was taking ahold of me and my life.

To top it off, in the midst of leading a homicide investigation and handling my other cases, I started gambling. I remember the day I became "addicted." The night before, my family and I had returned from vacation and while doing laundry my wife found a $100 bill. The following morning, wanting a much-needed break from my family, I told my wife that I was going to take the $100 and go to Mohegan Sun Casino to play blackjack. Wendy knew that I liked playing a few hands after we'd gone to a show or dinner and that it was always innocent fun. So when I asked her, it wasn't a big deal. I arrived at the casino with my $100 in hand, and within two hours I left with $900. I was ecstatic because I made an $800 profit in two hours and it would help to pay for my vacation bills. When I got home I gave Wendy eight 100 dollar bills and hung out with the family for a few hours. After dinner I went back to the Casino with my original $100 and turned that into $1,100 in two more hours. I couldn't believe how easy it was to count a few cards, stack a few bets, and walk away with a huge profit, all the while giving myself the biggest high I'd ever had.

Winning was always important to me, but winning money was indescribable. It was the highest of highs. Gambling quickly became a narcotic for me. When I lost, I needed to gamble even more. Like any addict, I was always searching for a greater high. The more I won, the better I felt. For the first few months I gambled, I handled it pretty well. I'd win a few hundred dollars here and there, and then I would lose it. When I ran out of my winnings I would stop betting and not use any of my personal money. As my depression worsened, however, I started gambling more often. Being depressed made me more susceptible to addictive behaviors like gambling and compulsive spending on toys and trips. This was the beginning of my downward spiral. I realized I had become addicted to gambling. Yes, that's right, I used the word addicted. Gambling was like a drug. When I wasn't gambling all I wanted to do was gamble. I thought about it at home, at work, when I was eating and when I was supposed to be sleeping. It consumed my life. I would lie to my wife and tell her I was working out at the barracks, when in reality I was using vacation days at work and sneaking off to the casino, trying to turn my $100 into $1000. I would take time off from work and run to the casino for a few hours before I was supposed to be home.

What most people don't realize is that once you've won money at any type of gambling (horse racing, sports betting, slot machines, and table games) your addiction has already taken hold of you. The second I won my first $800 I was done for. The casino had me in its grasp. It took me about a year and a half to realize that no matter how much money I won, I would always lose more than I took in. Unfortunately, the two largest casinos in the western hemisphere, Mohegan Sun and Foxwoods, were in my jurisdiction and a ten minute drive from my house.

Luckily, overall I didn't lose much money. In the year and a half that I was gambling I won about $8,000 and lost about $10,000. At the time, my wife and I were building a new house and I was the general contractor. I had access to $330,000. I was lucky. It could have been much worse financially.

When I was winning, my depression was fine. But when I lost, my depression worsened twofold. I would get a nauseating knot in the pit of my stomach after a loss. On those nights, on my way home from the casino, I would stop by McDonald's or Burger King and stuff ten dollars worth of shit into my mouth. Then I would arrive home and eat dinner with my family while attempting to hide the way I was feeling from my wife and kids.

I didn't tell Wendy about my gambling addiction until I was recuperating from rotator cuff surgery. As I was lying in bed under the influence of Oxycontin I told her that I needed her help. I explained what I had been doing for the past eighteen months. With her support I stopped gambling cold turkey. Deep down I had always known that if I didn't ask someone for help I was jeopardizing my family's well-being and risking the possibility of losing our new home. For whatever reason, subconsciously, in that sedated state, I decided to seek help from the person who loved me and cared for me the most, my wife Wendy. When I returned to work, instead of gambling, I refocused my attention on my job.

Chapter 11

This is John Patterson

One night my cousin John Bowen called and asked me to go out drinking with him and my other cousins, including Joe Buyak, to celebrate John's divorce being finalized. We met at one of their houses and then moved our party to a bar in Hartford. Whenever I go out I am always the designated drunk driver. I hate letting other people drive me around, especially when they have been drinking. I have a rule when I go out that limits how much I drink. I need to be able to fight, fuck and drive. I will drink the first half of the night and then drink water the second half so I can get everybody home safely. I don't drive intoxicated. At the end of this particular night my cousins drove me back to my car and asked me if I was okay to drive home, which I was. I told them that I was extremely tired because my infant daughter Amelia was keeping my wife and me up during the night, but I would make it home easily.

During my hour long drive, I started falling asleep at the wheel, and despite every attempt to keep myself awake, I evidently drove five to six miles completely asleep. When I awoke, I had lost control of my undercover State Police vehicle and had struck a guardrail in the center median of the highway. I had hit on the driver's side, so therefore the door was pinned and I was unable to open it. Being a good trooper, I turned on my State Police radio and advised the Troop F barracks that I had just been involved in a motor vehicle accident on the Interstate, and that I was uninjured. The funny thing was I actually crashed further down the highway in Troop E's area, Oops, so much for knowing where you are before you call in on the radio. Before the responding troopers arrived I telephoned my wife and told her that I had been in the accident, but was okay. Of course she asked me if I was drunk and I told her honestly that I was overtired and had fallen asleep. She called me an idiot and said she'd wait up for me to get home. The responding troopers investigated the accident and drove me home.

On Monday morning the big joke at the troop was that I had been drunk and crashed my state car. The Eastern District Major, John Rearick walked into the CI office at Troop E and said to me, "I heard you crashed your car this weekend."

In front of the entire office I responded, "I didn't crash my car, I crashed one of your fucking cars. Why would I crash my car?"

I've known Major Rearick since he was the commanding officer at the academy, so I felt comfortable being myself with him. In fact he is the only high ranking state police officer I respected. He paused for a moment, looked around the room, smiled and walked out of the office. As soon as his feet touched the hallway floor, the rest of the guys in the office started laughing their asses off. They couldn't believe that I had the balls to say that to a major in the almighty Connecticut State Police.

"Are you fucking nuts?" they asked. But they all knew that I was the type of person who wasn't shy about telling people what I was really thinking and that I was not going to tailor my personality just because I was speaking to somebody who had more authority than me. I said whatever was on my mind to whomever, whenever. I didn't pussy foot around anyone, and most people, especially my supervisors, hated that. The great thing about Major Rearick was that he didn't mind me being myself. It's funny, thinking back. I don't think I got written up for my accident.

With each new and troubling investigation, I took another negative shot to the brain. The only mechanism I had to deal with these problems was to laugh them off. I made fun of the children who were being raped and the assholes who perpetrated the crimes. Maybe the three year old asked to get sodomized, or maybe the seven year old girl just walked up to her father and started sucking his cock because she wanted to and she couldn't get enough of it. I know this sounds sick and it went against everything I believed in both morally and spiritually, but it helped me deal with this type of shit. It helped me survive.

We also started having rubber band fights in the Major Crime Squad office to relieve our tension and anger. If I remember correctly, I began this tradition. It might have been because I was as deadly shooting rubber bands, as I was shooting people. One day, the big guy in the office, Mr. Waffles (aka Bill Blanchette), grabbed his bowl of soup from the office microwave and started walking back toward his desk with smoke billowing from the hot broth. Unbeknownst to him, and with the detectives looking on, I pulled back two extremely thick rubber bands and hit him dead center in the back of his hand that was carrying the soup. I hit him so hard that his hand shook and the boiling broth went all over it. He started screaming like a bitch, but after a while he appreciated the humor of it all. Soon Mr. Waffles joined the rubber band wars and became quite skilled at it. Not as good as me though. At first we started hitting stationary targets on the walls or hanging from the office ceiling. One detective had a plastic chicken hanging from the ceiling by a string; I used to hit it three or four times a day. Then we graduated into hitting flying targets. We would throw shit into the air and try to hit it, or we would fly paper airplanes and try our luck at hitting them. Always, I was dead on.

Then we started hitting each others' hands. Mr. Waffles would hold his hand straight out to his side and I'd thwap him right in the middle of the inside of his palm. Of course when he wasn't looking I would tie two or three more rubber bands together to make it stronger and faster. It hurt like hell. I was accurate about 98.75% of the time, and he was accurate about 32%. That's why I liked playing the game with him. Soon we moved on to hitting each other on the top of the head. Whoever was the target would lower the top of his head toward the other and cover his eyes with his hands so no real injuries could occur. When you got hit on the top of your head it sounded as if someone punched a door. It was that loud. It hurt so bad it would make your eyes water. The other guys in the office would watch the entertainment of the day and chuckle whenever we hit each other. I think they liked me torturing Mr. Waffles.

Being a gentleman, I always gave Mr. Waffles the first opportunity to hit me, knowing full well that he'd miss and then I would hit whatever body part I aimed at. But he was a real good sport and kept playing, welts and all. If he said he wanted to quit, all I had to do was call him a pussy and he would stay in the game. In his defense though, he did have the best all-time shot in our rubber band fighting history. One of the area newspapers was writing a story about the effects the shootings had on me and they were taking pictures in our office for the article. I was sitting, posed for the camera, when Mr. Waffles hit me square nuts in the throat, causing me to cough and gasp for air. He laughed his balls off as I tried to find my voice-box on the floor behind me. The newspaper reporter turned around and looked at Mr. Waffles like he was fucking nuts. Waffles stopped laughing, looked at the reporter and simply said, "I'm sorry" and walked out of the office. I got the same look when I asked the camera man if he had gotten the shot as I was hit with the rubber band. I guess they didn't like, or quite understand, our humor.

We thought it was funny. It would have been a great photo.

Mr. Waffles and I would occasionally have a wrestling match in the middle of our office to release some steam. I would try to tackle him to the ground but he would roll me over and pin me for a moment until I got tired. He's got super strength and outweighs me by fifty pounds. Plus, I had two shoulder surgeries to boot. Sometimes Sergeant Rich or our Lieutenant would walk by the office while we were wrestling and just shake their heads and shut the door. These were just some of the things we would do to make the days go by more quickly and make our jobs a little less stressful.

I was also famous for dropping my trousers in the middle of the office for shits and giggles. I would pull my pants down to my ankles while the other guys were making serious phone calls, or I would place my hand on the corner of their desk and raise my ass in the air to make them laugh. One afternoon, when unbeknownst to me, Sergeant Rich was speaking with a reporter in his office that abutted the office bathroom, I decided to exit the bathroom with my pants down around my ankles. I opened the bathroom door and started shuffling my feet, slowly moving in the direction of my desk. I was wearing my American flag boxer briefs. As I shuffled a few feet down the hall, I turned to the left and saw the woman sitting in Sergeant Rich's office. She turned and looked at me with a blank stare in her eyes and her mouth wide open. Without skipping a beat, Sergeant Rich introduced me. "This is John Patterson." Having no other option, I bent over, pulled my pants up, made my apologies, and walked back to my desk, and into the arms of a laughing Detective Ted Parker.

Teddy is a cerebral assassin. He was the smartest detective in the office as well as extremely funny. He was well known for his David Copperfield-like trick, known as The Bubbler. The Bubbler was an optical illusion that he created when he pissed at such an angle, height and distance that it appeared as if he were drinking his own pee. It was great entertainment. He could piss farther and higher than anyone I had ever seen. I think he could have actually pissed over one of those '70s VW buses without getting a drop on it.

Teddy was also known for pulling off the greatest practical joke in our office history with another detective, Steve Rief. One of our detectives, Paul Gately, had met a police officer from Louisiana at a police training course and agreed to send him a Connecticut State Police

Stetson hat. Paul brought the hat to the office, boxed and ready to mail. While Paul was away from his desk, Steve opened the box using his knife with surgical precision, removed the brand new hat from the box and exchanged the new hat with an older, well-worn State Police hat. But not before Teddy had thrown it on the ground, stomped on it, and written STATE POLICE on the front with magic marker. Steve and Teddy resealed the box, and when Paul returned to the office he sent the supposed new hat off to his new friend in the fine state of Louisiana. A few weeks later we were sitting at our desks when Paul got a phone call. We heard Paul getting really upset and could see his face turning redder and redder. He started yelling things like "What the fuck are you talking about?" and "What do you mean? The hat was brand new!" It dawned on us that Paul was speaking with the officer from Louisiana. Teddy started laughing, grabbed the real hat and threw it on Paul's desk. Paul laughed as he tried to convince the Louisiana officer that it was all a big joke. When Paul got off the phone he looked at Teddy and Steve and told them that they had gotten him good. Of course we all wanted to know what the Louisiana officer had said. Paul told us that he asked him if what he sent him was a big joke and that after describing to Paul what kind of condition the hat was in, the officer said "I'm so pissed off that I'm sitting in a pile of my own shit!" Must have been a Louisiana thing.

Although our office was like a show on Comedy Central at times, we were the busiest and hardest working detective unit in the Connecticut State Police. While other officers were getting called out two or three times a month in the middle of the night, our office was getting called out two to three times a week. Every untimely and unexplained death had to be investigated by us. With every one of these deaths came the autopsy. I've been to countless autopsies over the years and each one of them has affected me in a negative way. Seeing a dead body is never easy, but smelling one is inexplicably difficult. It's definitely not as cool as it is portrayed on television.

As soon as I walk into the room where autopsies are performed, I'm hit with a waft of air that smells of death. There is no other smell on earth that comes close to that of a dead person. It is indescribable and unexplainable. It's an odd putrid smell. No one can understand what I'm talking about unless they've smelled another dead human being. The Medical Examiner's Office handles all of the autopsies in Connecticut, so whenever I have the pleasure of visiting the ME's office for an autopsy there are multiple autopsies going on. Someone is sawing the tops off of two or three heads, or pulling the intestines out of their bodies. It's great stuff. Then they throw all the innards in a black garbage bag, place it into the cadaver's open chest cavity and sew the chest back up. The hardest time for me is when they wheel out a dead kid and start going through the motions. I turn the other way and make it a point never to look at the autopsy of a small child or young teen. Anything having to do with kids freaks me out.

I had one experience in the Medical Examiner's office that I consider to be extremely funny, in a sick and twisted kind of way. One morning Detective Jay Masson and I were asked to go to an autopsy for some poor dead slob. When we walked into the meat locker where the slaughters (my take on autopsies) take place, Jay and I saw a few other detectives in the room dressed in all their protective gear. When most people attend an autopsy they put protective clothing and booties over their clothes and shoes so they don't get any blood or brain matter on themselves. I've been to so many autopsies that I just walk in and do what I need to do in the clothes I am wearing.

On this day I was taking the requisite pictures of the body I was investigating when one of the ME workers rolled another body out of the refrigerator. It was a big fat green-colored man in a one piece woman's bathing suit. As soon as I saw the guy I yelled Holy shit—it's Shrek. Everyone in the room started laughing except for one female intern who covered her mouth with her hand and ran out of the room, probably to throw up. I swear to God, the guy looked like and was the same exact color as Shrek. It was such a likeness that I gave Jay the camera I was using and asked him to take a picture of me standing next to dead Shrek. Before he could snap the picture, my smarter mind prevailed and we didn't take it. We found out that Shrek had slipped on his wife's one piece bathing suit after she left for the weekend and climbed into their hot tub. When the wife returned three days later, she found him floating in the hot tub, dead. Apparently if you sit in a hot tub for three days straight you turn the color green. This remains one of Jay's and my favorite stories.

While I was out on medical leave after the first incident, my barrack's commander, Lieutenant Munster, kept bugging me to come back to work. He would call me at home and ask how I was doing, and he would end the conversation every time by asking me when I was coming back on the job. In my opinion, Lieutenant Munster believed wholeheartedly that if he acted as if he cared about me, I would believe him and respect him for it, but he was the guy who would hug you and say, Hi Brother, then turn around and jam an ice pick in your back if he didn't like you. He never had the balls to discipline someone face to face; he would tell a sergeant to do his dirty work for him. He thought he was smarter than everybody else, but everyone saw through his bullshit. When I returned to work after my first shooting, Lieutenant Munster actually banned me from attending roll call at Troop E because I would address problems troopers were having at the barracks level with a sergeant or with Munster at roll call. He didn't like subordinates standing up to him, and God forbid, standing up to him in front of a roomful of subordinates. So I was never in a hurry to tell him I'd be back.

During my stint in the Criminal Investigation Unit, Lieutenant Munster continued to hound me to come back to work with him. The CI office was directly across from his office, so it was easy for him to get to me. After the shooting, Lieutenant Munster temporarily placed a patrol trooper in Jewett City until my return. That meant paying another trooper overtime to fill the vacant patrol position, and he was concerned he would be questioned about the overtime he was using. It had always been his practice to return overtime hours monthly, so he would look good in the eyes of the District Major. He prided himself in doing this, but it was at the expense of his troopers. By not filling certain overtime shifts, he sacrificed the safety of his troopers to look good to top management. This disgusted me and caused me to hate him to the core. He bothered me so much while I was in the Criminal Investigations Unit that I called the Employee Assistance Program and told them I needed to go out on disability or leave work because of the amount of undue stress Lieutenant Munster was causing me. Ultimately, I went out on worker's compensation for about six weeks until the Internal Affairs and State's Attorney's investigations were completed. Once I was out on Worker's Compensation Lieutenant Munster didn't bother me again.

Chapter 12

Tap, tap, tappity, tap

Shortly after the second shooting I was given the name of a clini-cal psychologist with experience counseling police officers who had been involved in police related shootings. All my defense mechanisms, macabre humor and near insubordination weren't enough to deal with what I was feeling.

Wanting to stop the recurring dreams and nightmares I had been having since the incident, I decided to make the appointment. The psychologist's name was Doctor Mark Hall. But thinking about it and doing it were two different things. It took me a couple of months to take that leap. Like an addict, I first had to admit that I had a problem and then I had to make the decision to get the help I desperately needed. Making that decision to seek counseling was the hardest part of this long process for me; because it was an admission of vulnerability and weakness. And there it is. The last thing I ever wanted to admit.

After my first shooting, when Jay Gaughan and I met with the State Police psychiatrist, we came away with the belief that he and I were sane and the psychiatrist was nuts. We laughed at his attempts to impart his wisdom. I had also seen a female psychiatrist for a few appointments after the first shooting but was unable to make a pos-itive and healthy connection with her. It was hard for me to tell her the details of the shooting or aspects of the other incidents I had been involved in because she was a woman. When I would attempt to work through the traumatic events, I could tell from her facial expression that she was uncomfortable hearing the details, and that was a turn-off for me. She also incorporated a new therapy technique called Eye Movement Desensitization and Reprogramming (EMDR), which was quite awkward. She would have me follow her finger with my eyes as she moved it left and right while I was working through an issue. My understanding was that the rapid eye movement would desensitize my memory of the issue at hand. I laughed it off as a form of voodoo and didn't take it seriously. I came to understand that my age and immatu-rity had a lot to do with that reaction. I hoped Dr. Hall would be differ-ent; I had no other alternatives.

Around that same time a retired local police officer, Arthur Kurec-zka, began a support group for police officers who had been involved in critical incidents. Art was a retired Wethersfield officer who was involved in a police shooting in the 1980s. He started the support group so officers could speak with one another about their critical incidents, and the negative affect at home and work. Art believed the support group would be a nice prelude into full-time counseling for the affected officers. It was a fantastic idea. The group met once a month and dis-cussed on-going issues. There were eight to ten faithful attendees, including Art. One third of the members had been involved in police related shootings and the other two thirds had been adversely affected by horrific crime scenes or fatal accidents they had seen.

During the first few meetings each officer would tell the group what they had been through and what they were hoping to get out of the support group. It was funny to me because every officer was having the same problems I was. Everyone, in their introduction to the support group, said "I hate people!" None of the officers were getting any support from their department. All of them were lethargic and unmotivated at work and were overall sad and depressed. Most indicated they were fighting with their spouses more often, due to their disconnected feel-ings toward the world around them. Up until this point, I believed I was the only police officer in the state of Connecticut who was dealing with these problems. But here were other officers who had been affected as much as I had been. The support group assured me I wasn't alone. There was a commonality between us. Although the group fizzled out after a few years, I believe that the group prepared me to reach out for assistance from Dr. Hall.

After a few months in the group, I finally got the courage to call Dr. Hall. The whole individual counseling thing was a bit strange for me at first. It was weird sitting across from a stranger and telling him my life story and why I believed I needed help. Staring at someone for fifty minutes and maybe talking for ten of them was awkward and uncom-fortable at best. However, once I allowed myself to let go and trust him, it became easier. With each visit I was able to open up and talk more. But first I had to realize that Dr. Hall was there to listen and help.

As it became easier over time to talk with Dr. Hall, I began to work through a number of the problems I was having at home and work. Dr. Hall provided positive feedback and healthy advice regarding whatever issues I presented in the session. He was good at communicating different coping skills and explaining ways of working through issues. I spent a good deal of time processing my nightmares in therapy. When I described a horrific dream to Dr. Hall he would ask, "Why do you think that happened?" or "What did you think the significance of that was?" Then he would sit back and listen to me work my way through the dream. Over time I was able to understand the significance of the dream and its imagery. Eventually Dr. Hall and I decided that instead of seeing him once every two weeks, as I had been doing, I could see him once every few months or when a problem in my life arose and I felt that I needed help to process it.

Therapy sessions with Dr. Hall helped me to understand the reasons for my depression and what I needed to do to actively combat it. He also helped me to recognize how my depression affected my wife and children, which was what concerned me the most. Even though I made a conscious effort to be aware of the signs of my depression before any issues ensued, it didn't always work. Most of the time I didn't realize what I was doing to negatively impact my family. Every so often Wendy would call Dr. Hall and set up an appointment for both of us so we could discuss what she thought my issues were. My problems were always the same. I was tired all of the time, I didn't want to go anywhere in public or attend parties where there were a lot of people, and overall I was just sad. I drank more and only sporadically worked out, which caused my self-esteem to plummet. When something shitty happened at work or when I got into an argument with Wendy I would head for the Drive-Thru at McDonald's and eat ten dollars worth of fast, or should I say, fat food. When I got into this state of lethargy my wife would say "I know you shot and killed two people, but you have a beautiful family and you need to get over it." The problem with my wife's well-intentioned, but ultimately thoughtless and insensitive comment was simply that I couldn't. The depression was bigger than me. The shootings changed me forever and I will never be the same person I was before. I think she wants back the person she married; the life of the party who would make everyone laugh at all costs. It saddens me to admit that this will never happen.

I was prescribed Zoloft, Paxil and Cymbalta for my depression, but they never really worked. I hoped that one of the medications would boost my energy, but they all seemed to sap it. I was always tired. Dr.

Hall and Wendy thought my mood was better and I seemed brighter when I was taking the medications, but I couldn't see it. So I stopped taking them. I haven't taken any medications for the past several years, and it has been a battle. I'm not against taking drugs; I just wish I could take something to boost my energy. Every time I see Dr. Hall I ask him for an upper, like speed. I've done some research and thought about taking Human Growth Hormone (HGH), but I can't find a doctor to prescribe it for me. It's not like I'm training to be a body builder. I just need something to give me that boost.

A few years into therapy Dr. Hall suggested I try EMDR again. He was aware of my past experience with this method of therapy, but he thought I was more mature and more open to using any and all therapeutic methods to cure my depression. He also told me the process had been modified and no longer used the finger technique. They discovered EMDR worked not because you moved your eyes back and forth, but because by moving your eyes, you were accessing both sides of the brain in rapid succession. This right brain/left brain activity was what allowed traumatic stored memories to be accessed and reprocessed. Now you get your brain working in this way by holding "tappers", small hand-held electronic devices that vibrate like the pagers you get in a restaurant when you are waiting to be called to the table. The therapist alternates the intensity and timing of the bi-lateral vibrations to facilitate your mind going back and forth between right brain and left brain.

I agreed to try EMDR again and over a twelve week period I went through the process. During the first few sessions, Dr. Hall and I discussed the ten things in my life that disturbed me the most. My list included the death of my grandmother in a plane crash in Alaska, my mother's diagnosis of breast cancer, the night my wife and I learned her teenage brother had been killed in an automobile accident and my two shootings. Each week I was given the tappers to hold and while they were vibrating I discussed each event in great detail, working through them as they occurred. As I replayed each event in my mind, I explained it out loud. It felt to me as if I was sort of hypnotized. After working through a particular event the therapist would tell me to go to my happy place before we discussed what had occurred during the EMDR session.

Anyone who knows me probably thinks that my happy place was similar to Happy Gilmore's happy place (Tap, Tap, Tappity, Tap), but in reality the place I would go to in my mind was Cinnamon Bay, a beautiful beach in St. John, US Virgin Islands.

Working through each event with EMDR enabled me to free my mind. Any issues I had previous to my two shootings were gone. This made it easier for me to work through each shooting effectively. A very healing moment came while discussing one of the shootings. I cried during this session, then apologized for breaking down. It was out of character for me to cry and I was more embarrassed than anything. I hadn't really cried since right after the second shooting when I broke down at the scene and when I cried at my moms house after Wendy sent me packing. But while driving home it seemed as if a huge weight had been lifted off my shoulders. It was like having a bad head cold with a stuffy nose. You feel like shit so you take a thirty minute steaming hot shower and all the nasty stuff that was built up in your nose and sinuses drains from your head, allowing you to breathe freely. That's what I felt like driving home. For the first time in a long time I felt relief and an overwhelming feeling of inner peace. I felt like I was born again and that things would be getting better. Since using EMDR as a therapy tool, I have had only a handful of nightmares. That left only the problem of my lethargy.

After my first shooting I had set goals for myself to make myself work out. In late 1996 and early 1997 Harold French (Frenchy) and I became interested in the World Police and Fire Games. These games are the second largest sporting event in the world, after the Olympics; with roughly 8,000 police officers and fire fighters competing. Ultimately, I competed in five World Games in Calgary, Canada; Stockholm, Sweden; Indianapolis, Indiana; New York City; and Barcelona, Spain.

I boxed in both Sweden and Spain. At first boxing was a tool I used to keep myself in shape. But soon after I started, I absolutely fell in love with it. It was not only good for my body, but it was good for my mind. It made me a stronger person, both physically and mentally. It taught me to be self-reliant and reinforced the fact that I could handle myself when I needed to. Boxing also kept my ego in check and it helped to build self-confidence in a way no other sport could. Getting my ass kicked by a 135 pound, fifteen year old Hispanic kid, or trading punches with a light heavyweight champion was humbling. Boxing was therapeutic for me and helped me deal with my own tragedies. I was able to get my fat ass down to a fighting weight of 176 pounds for the light heavyweight division, from 196 pounds.

Since my second shooting it has been a constant battle to stay active and physically fit. From the time I was in high school I had prided myself in lifting weights and running to keep in shape. When I graduated the State Police Academy in 1993, at the age of twenty-two, I weighed 165 pounds and had a 32" waist. Now, at the age of forty-three, my weight fluctuates between 195 and 205 pounds and I have a 36" waist. I'm in decent shape and by no means am I fat, but a healthy weight for me would be 185 pounds. When my gun belt and pants get too tight, I eat right, work out a little harder and get back to where I need to be.

That's what twenty plus years as a police officer has done for me. Work out, don't work out, eat like shit, work out, eat like shit, don't work out, work out, eat like shit etc. etc. etc. It's become a never-ending cycle.

Staying active and physically fit throughout my depression was hard to do. I treated working out as if it were a job. Some days I wanted to go to the gym and other days I didn't. I looked for every excuse in the book to not exercise. That was one of the reasons I was tired so much of the time. I used the I'm too tired to work out today excuse all of the time. But overall, in the years since my second shooting it's been a constant battle to come up with new challenges to keep me active and healthy. Like dealing with my depression, it is a continual struggle.

What I've known all along, but have only recently embraced, is that working out boosts my energy and makes me feel less depressed. My attitude has slowly changed from I'm too tired to work out, so don't— to— I know I'm tired, but I have to work out because I'll feel better. Changing my mind set has been effective and now I work out on a regular basis. But my battle with depression will never end or subside. I have to live day by day and adapt to whatever obstacles are presented in either my personal or professional life. It's survival of the fittest. As long as I stay fit, I will survive!

Chapter 13

Interview with Dr. Mark Hall
by Deborah L. Mandel

"It is not the case, like in the movies, that cops shoot people all the time. The cops I have talked to feel very uncomfortable pulling their guns. It is really unusual and unique to have this happen twice."
Dr. Mark Hall

I have known Dr. Hall, personally and professionally, for many years. Dr. Hall is a clinical psychologist in private practice in Glastonbury, Connecticut. Prior to opening his practice he worked for 11 years at the Traumatic Stress Institute (TSI) in South Windsor. At TSI he developed a specialty in treating adults who had experienced psychological trauma resulting from abuse, war, accidents, and law-enforcement incidents. He was part of TSI's effort to develop a theory of the impact of psychological trauma, a theory which continues to shape Dr. Hall's clinical approach. His private practice currently consists of a large number of municipal police officers and state troopers referred to him after being involved in on-the-job shootings or other high-stress experiences. In addition, he works with the State Police Computer Crimes Unit on an on-going basis, helping their staff manage the stresses of daily exposure to child pornography.

Therapy for John, while successful in the long run, did not come easily. Police officers, out of necessity, develop a thick skin to shield them from the daily barrage of difficult and dangerous situations they encounter. This obdurate exterior can offset symptoms of PTSD temporarily, but not forever. By the time John entered therapy, life had become unmanageable, both personally and professionally. John entered treatment with Dr. Hall in September 2000, four years following the first shooting, and almost two years after the second shooting.

During his first meeting with Dr. Hall, John described himself as a blunt, outspoken asshole. "He almost prided himself in that," Dr. Hall said. This offensive play, on John's part, reflected an intrinsic part of his personality, which enabled him to down play and avoid the internal emotional turmoil that had developed as a result of the trauma he had experienced. John said he had flat affect (no visible emotional response) and was stoic before these events happened, but had become much more so after the second shooting.

By the time John entered therapy he was experiencing symptoms of PTSD. He had frequent nightmares related to the incidents, he suffered from acute lethargy and depression (especially since the second shooting), and held a strong belief that nothing really mattered any more. Earlier in his career John was the officer who would go out there and make the arrest. He could be counted on by his peers to show up and do whatever was needed to be done in a situation. Now he had no drive or initiative at work. His life outside of work was equally affected. He had lost interest in things that had previously been important to him and was unenthusiastic about everything he was doing. Friends had gone by the wayside. He had quit working out and stopped competing in organized sports events, which resulted in significant weight gain. This was a man who had prided himself on entering the Toughest Competitor Alive (TCA) competition in the WPFG, not caring about how well he did, or how beat up he got. He loved the demanding nature of the event. John was also experiencing memory and word retrieval problems. Significant marital tribulations had arisen with his wife Wendy.

After the first shooting, John explained, he had been able to compartmentalize the experience, tuck it away and go on with his life. In part he attributed this to the fact that he was there with his partner and it was clear what needed to be done. The assailant was either going to kill them or himself and would not respond to verbal commands to stop. Both he and his partner made the decision to shoot simultaneously, which gave John a sense of validation.

John's reaction to the second shooting was more intense without the benefit of that validation. John was working alone and had to make all decisions on his own. Disbelief that this was happening to him again added to the already frightening and potentially life-threatening experience. Also compounding the difficulty of the situation was the fear that his backup officer, and life-long friend, Stowell, was in danger. The threat to one's own life or to someone else's is the major cause of the development of PTSD. Both were going on for John at this time.

"It is not the case, like in the movies, that cops shoot people all the time. The cops I have talked to feel very uncomfortable pulling their guns. It is really unusual and unique to have this happen twice," Dr. Hall remarked.

John's lethargy continued throughout much of his treatment. He experienced significant difficulty accessing his feelings as well as trusting that he could depend on other people. However, during more than one session he acknowledged how much sadness he carried around. Some of this sadness centered on his spirituality. John expressed conflict about being Catholic and having killed someone, claiming he would need two hours of Hail Mary's to get forgiveness (John's humor covering his innate fear). Catholic boys are not supposed to kill people. As a child, John had been very involved with the church, and served for many years as an altar boy. As an adult he had been experiencing some disenchantment with the Church because of the sexual abuse perpetrated by the priests, including speculation about the priest that he best knew in the neighborhood. After the shootings this conflict presented a real struggle.

In therapy John focused on his suspicion of and blanket hatred for people. As with many police officers, John had lost faith in the public; they were always lying to him and trying to trick him. He dealt with the worst people, constantly exposed to their meanness, sadism, self-centeredness. The men and women he saw were living on the margins, using drugs, involved in domestic disputes or rapes. He spent his working hours with individuals who were unable or unwilling to make the right decisions and who were abusive to others. As with many in his profession, this put John on the defensive and he began to generalize from these perpetrators to everyone—the world was bad. In doing this John could bury the tender parts of himself, in order to protect them. This is a common element of burnout that is seen among officers, where the negative aspects of people become over generalized. Because of his extreme distaste for people, John began to dislike and avoid situations in which a lot of people were involved, such as parties or other social events. These particular issues created significant turmoil in his marriage. Wendy wished he could be more open socially. Wendy and John met with Dr. Hall on numerous occasions to help her understand the impact of PTSD as well as to negotiate strategies for working on their relationship. With two, and then later three, young children, his symptoms would at times present an overwhelming strain on their marriage.

Aside from these meetings with Wendy, John met weekly with Dr.

Hall for individual 50 minute sessions to work on the issues relating to his PTSD and depression. For those not familiar with the therapeutic process, the format is fairly straight forward. John would come to sessions and talk about both current and past events. Dr. Hall would help John to understand how the PTSD had developed and teach him strategies to deal with it. In PTSD therapy, one important treatment procedure is to talk over, repeatedly, the precipitating incidents in order to understand and get a handle on the emotional fallout. As was true with John, feelings and reactions are often buried and these drive the subsequent depression and anxiety. To this end, there was a period of time in therapy where John repeatedly listened to a tape of the dispatcher's call from the second shooting. "The thing that struck me the most about that [tape] was the moment when you could hear John's own fear and vulnerability," said Dr. Hall. John worried that it was weird or pathological that he wanted to listen to this tape, but Dr. Hall encouraged him to follow his inclinations. As long as the tapes did not aggravate his symptoms, listening to the tapes would be helpful in dealing with his feelings from that night. In fact it was therapeutically useful and they used the tape in their work together. It cannot be overstated that directly confronting the feelings about the precipitating event is very helpful in PTSD treatment. For John to listen to the tape, and hear his fear, allowed him to dispel the grip of terror it held over him.

Dr. Hall taught John relaxation techniques, a useful tool in helping individuals access their feelings, by creating an inner safe place to go if feelings become overwhelming. When John practiced relaxation he would visualize himself at the beach at Cinnamon Bay in St. John, U.S. Virgin Islands, his favorite vacation spot. As Cinnamon Bay beach became a safe haven he could go to when experiencing difficulty, John allowed himself to delve deeper into his feelings. Without this backup, it can be very distressing for individuals with PTSD to revisit the trauma. While this proved helpful, John's depressive symptoms continued and with much reluctance he eventually agreed to go on some antidepressants. According to Dr. Hall, John frequently went on and off the medications, and he never really knew if John was taking them. "I think he was getting some benefits from them; however, I am not sure he ever did it for a significant length of time," said Dr. Hall. This resistance to taking medication is not unusual as it challenges the belief that the individual is strong enough to do it on his own.

As a result of John's continued difficulty in opening up and allowing himself to express his feelings, Dr. Hall brought in a colleague to do
Eye Movement Desensitization and Reprocessing (EMDR) with John.
EMDR is a therapy technique that integrates elements from various
therapeutic modalities; psychodynamic, cognitive, behavioral, inter-
personal, experiential and body centered. It is a theory which attempts
to explain how information is perceived, stored and retrieved, as well
as how to most effectively treat PTSD and acute stress. It is a well-re-
searched treatment protocol; its effectiveness documented in multiple
controlled studies (EMDR Institute, Inc., www.emdr.com). Its use is
recommended by the American Psychiatric Association, The Departments of Defense and Veteran Affairs and the International Society for
Traumatic Stress Studies for dealing with PTSD and related symptoms
such as intrusive thoughts, numbing, hyper-arousal, grief and depression.

Developed by Francine Shapiro in the early 1990's, EMDR has
become a well-recognized avenue of treatment. Using rapid eye movements (or tapping) the client's external focus is directed outward, while
internal focus is directed to the traumatic material. This dual focus is
fundamental to the process although not completely understood. There
are multiple theories about how and why it works, the consensus being
that there is some neurobiological process occurring.

Shapiro (1995) hypothesized that there is an inherent information
processing system in which learning happens and memory is stored.
These information networks contain thoughts, images, emotions and
sensations. If a traumatic event is not thoroughly processed, then the
memories are stored in their original traumatic state— causing the
intrusive thoughts and emotions, which in turn cause the dysfunc-
tional state of PTSD. Reprocessing the event and linking it with more
adaptive information allows for forward movement out of the trapped
memories. For example, if someone was in a car accident in which their
child was injured, they might believe that they were responsible for the
injury because they had not stepped on the brake fast enough, thus
holding onto a negative belief about the event. EMDR would help the
person develop a more realistic understanding—that they stepped on
the brake as fast as they could, but the accident was out of their control.
In very simplistic terms, by experiencing the emotional impact of the
accident and the child's injury, and pairing it with the realization that

they were not responsible, the trauma symptoms can be resolved.

This therapeutic technique, frequently used with war veterans, rape victims and other traumatized individuals, provided a way for John to connect with his feelings, and to pull out some of the emotional themes. EMDR softened John in a way that nothing else had and he benefited from those sessions. The psychologist began by having John go through some of the most difficult events in his life. She did not begin with the shootings, but worked up to them, starting with earlier life situations. As he worked through these experiences one by one, the affect associated with them was greatly reduced. He finally worked through the shootings, and the impact of the ensuing trial.

The father of the man killed in the second shooting filed a law suit against John and the state police, claiming John took his child away from him. While John was on the stand, the civil rights attorney questioning him was provocative, making comments to the effect that because this has happened twice, John must enjoy killing people. He accused John of being a murderer. This tapped into John's despair at having killed someone, justified or not, and he became enraged at the lawyer. He agonized over his belief that good Christians do not kill; therefore he must not be a good Christian. John realized he had to stay cool and could not lash out at the attorney. It was a challenge to sit on the stand and remain calm. The irony was that at the same time this lawyer was accusing John of being murderous, John's internal feeling was murderous—toward the lawyer for treating him so badly. The EMDR helped him reduce a significant amount of this rage.

The EMDR relaxed John and helped him access a lot of the sadness he felt regarding the two shooting incidents. It also allowed him to realize that he had been expecting himself to be God-like. Over the course of several sessions, John came to the understanding that he was not in fact invincible, nor should he expect himself to be. He faced the realistic limits of his own power.

One technique used in EMDR therapy is to have the client engage in an internal dialogue between different aspects of his inner self. We all have different inner parts, which we use in different life circumstances. Who we are as parents is different from who we are as friends and different from who we are internally. John was able to hold a dialogue between his core self and the part of him that is a state trooper. In this conversation, which focused on the period of time prior to engaging with the man in the second shooting incident, John was able to see that the trooper part of him was scared. He was then able to reassure this trooper aspect of himself that it was normal to be afraid in such an extreme situation. The trooper part was helped by these assurances, but in return, his trooper-self impressed upon John that a shooting could happen again. This was one of the reasons John listened to the tape of his calls to the station, to remind himself to be alert; it could happen again.

A powerful moment occurred during the EMDR treatment when John realized that he identified with the children from the first shooting, who had been playing in their yard, next door to, and across the street from, the suspect, when the suspect came charging out of his house with a knife. John's immediate reaction had been to get the children to a safe place. He became very emotional during this session and felt very good about having protected them, realizing that he too had an inner six-year-old child that needed protection. John was accepting and not critical about recognizing this part of him; he consoled his inner six-year-old, reaching below that usual tough guy demeanor to do so. It was an important step for John to identify himself as a young boy who longed for solace, protection and comfort. He felt betrayed by God and by his Church. He confronted the reality that he did what he had to do in very unusual circumstances, and was able to forgive himself and have compassion for the young boy who had betrayed the morals and ethics of the church. He accepted as well that it was okay to need comforting as an adult, especially when dealing with such extreme experiences.

As part of therapy, John focused on phrases like "I did what I had to do" and "I wish this didn't happen," which led to more of an acceptance of what had transpired. He was able to acknowledge his sadness about the shootings and all that he had seen in his line of work.

I think about John "as the guy who goes out and slays the dragon for the community, then comes back emotionally and maybe physically scarred," Dr. Hall said, "but that is the price that he pays, that is his identity." This was another of the major themes that ran throughout treatment, John's perception of himself as The Protector. In fact, this idea of being The Protector formed a large piece of John's conflict. He realized that by being a cop he ran the risk of an officer coming to his front door and reporting to his wife that he had been killed—which is very close to what happened. An officer did come to the house to tell

Wendy that he had been involved in a shooting. The magnitude of this was not lost on John.

Therein lies the conflict. John is out there protecting the world, or his partner, or children in harm's way; yet doing so puts his family in very real danger of losing him. For John, personally, it is a worthwhile price to pay, putting himself in danger and carrying the memories of having lived through that danger, because he is protecting other people.

John has a new role now in the department; he is a two time shooter. John is the experienced hero in the eyes of his fellow officers and he both likes and dislikes the role. If there is a tough situation on the road everyone says, "John is the one who should have been here for this." In his work with Dr. Hall, they explored the question of whether this made him a hero or a sacrificial lamb.

"John is a hero who could not fully be a part of his own family as he was busy being a dispensable protector: who is outside but not fully connected to the ones he is protecting," said Dr. Hall "To me this is the Achilles Heel of the hero, focusing on the well-being of others and making you dispensable in the process." Inevitably this makes for varied needs that erupt in some fashion; longings that don't get fulfilled.

Another issue that ran through therapy was John's feeling that due to his PTSD he should have qualified for retirement disability. At that time PTSD was not a widely accepted diagnosis for police officers. But the fact that John saw other officers get a lot more attention and a lot more benefits for much lesser things, created resentment. However, John's style got in the way of his being seen as someone who needed to be retired. Anyone looking at John would see someone out there doing his job. He was not falling apart, and he was not really complaining. He would go out there in his own stoic way to do what needed to be done. The hurt and pain he carried inside was not obvious to his co-workers. If John went to a disability hearing, they would say that his performance ratings were high and that he was doing his job very effectively. John could have made a case for PTSD, though, had he wanted. He checked it out and talked to the union attorney, but did not pursue it.

John's dreams were a good indicator of what was going on internally in his process. Recurrent nightmares about the trauma are common in PTSD. In John's dreams he was either shooting at someone or being shot at. An interesting development in therapy was the change in the emotional context of these dreams. In his earliest dreams he wasn't getting shot, he was the shooter. Over time the dreams changed to ones where he was not able to protect himself, not able to assemble his gun in time. The emotional trauma evident in these dreams represented John's overwhelming sense of powerlessness. John's emotional trauma had been due in part to his sense of helplessness. Midway through therapy he had a dream in which he had a bullet wound in his head that others were looking at, but he was walking around as if normal. "Here he had a wound that was so obvious to everyone but he could not see it; a very representative dream," said Dr. Hall.

In January '04, on the sixth and eighth year anniversary of the two shootings, John had an especially frightening dream where he again was unable to shoot a perpetrator. Instead the man shot and killed him and John saw himself lying in a coffin. While in most ways the dreams had gotten better, this was a blip on the screen, an especially frightening dream. The dream began with him fumbling with the gun and then progressed to him being shot, not knowing he was shot and then being buried, playing out the scenario of his worst fear. "Maybe this was the fear being played out of him dying," said Dr. Hall, "the fear being played out in his dream." Over the course of treatment the distress decreased in the dreams and the frequency of the dreams was reduced as well. He would, however, have a resurgence of dreams around the anniversary of the shootings, or when anything provoked memories of what happened. Nightmares about the events leading to PTSD are generally the hardest symptom to eradicate.

Dr. Hall would frequently discuss the impact of John's job, not only in regard to the shootings, but in terms of all the work he had done. John had worked as a detective doing sexual assault investigations and he had worked on the road. He had seen a lot of horrific situations. According to John, the incidents involving children were the worst. He carried around a huge well of sadness in him, about children who were hurt or injured. He had processed a lot of rapes, seen a lot of sexual assaults. Carrying this burden is true for a lot of officers. They don't really know what to do with the emotion, it is so big that they can't really touch it, and there's no place to go with it. The general expectation is to suck it up.

Due to this unspoken code, John often stayed on the surface, seeing feelings as weakness. This contributed to his difficulty in accessing his emotions or trusting that he could depend on other people. He expressed the belief that only when he retired would he allow himself the luxury of laying down the tough demeanor that served him well as a cop. He talked numerous times about his fear of losing his edge, if he let himself feel his feelings. "In my opinion," said Dr. Hall, "if you can regulate it, that would be good. If when you go home, you could hang it up with your keys, that would be ideal. But that's easy to say and a lot harder to do."

A final area that John worked on with Dr. Hall centered on his early comments about himself—that he was a blunt, outspoken asshole. John had difficulty in knowing when to state his mind and when to keep quiet. "John prides himself on taking on the brass," said Dr. Hall. "He has a particular contempt for people in leadership roles that are not acting in respectable ways and he feels no conflict about sassing them, or talking back, especially after the two shootings." He figured that there was nothing left they could do to him. There was a righteousness about him, like he was on a mission and his response was utterly justified." Obviously, this did not always sit well with his superiors.

In later sessions John noticed that there was a shift in his ability to hold back in this area. There would be a meeting at work, and John would be conscious of how long he would wait before he said something. This skill spilled over into his personal life. John was aware that even outside of work he was holding back more, and making fewer comments.

Despite his ups and downs, his initial resistance to delve below the surface, and the often overwhelming symptoms of PTSD, John did get better over time. While the lethargy and the lack of enthusiasm were the hardest aspects to reverse, his mood lightened a little bit after a while. He began to participate in activities he had previously enjoyed, like exercising. He got back into life more. Wendy reported that he seemed more present than he had been. But life was not always smooth. There was a time when he was in between houses with a new baby, and he became more depressed again. Once they moved into their new home and life got simpler, things settled down and he settled down as well. His relationship with Wendy became more stable. For individuals with PTSD, symptoms can reoccur when new, albeit unrelated, stresses appear. This is to be expected. John will always need to be aware that turmoil may be a trigger for him. He must watch for signs of depression or anxiety when life is in any sort of upheaval. He continues to periodically see Dr. Hall when the need arises; but he has come a long way from the emotional mayhem he was experiencing when he first entered therapy.

Chapter 14

Crying on TV

In late September 1999 the Attorney General's Office of Connecticut notified me I was being sued by Joseph Parsons' father in federal court for civil rights violations. On October 7, 1999 I was deposed and provided a sworn affidavit concerning the shooting. The deposition went smoothly and I didn't have any increase in depressive symptoms or negative thoughts. At the deposition, I learned from my attorney, Steve Sarnowski, that Mr. Parsons had retained John R. Williams, a civil rights attorney who had represented the Black Panthers during the 1960s. Although at the time I didn't know much about Attorney Williams, I figured that he would try to sensationalize the shooting and place the blame squarely on my shoulders. My gut feelings proved to be right, although at the time I had no idea just how right they would be. I was told that it would take a year or two for the lawsuit to go forward and make it to federal court.

A few days later I was contacted by Pete Curley who ran the Public Safety Employee Assistance Program (EAP) for our department. Pete asked me, on behalf of the Commissioner of the State Police, to speak to the Governor's Law Enforcement Council about my shootings. The council was asked by then-Governor John Rowland to look into recent police shootings in an attempt to study whether or not police in Connecticut were using deadly force too often. The council was also tasked with determining whether or not the investigations into these shootings were thorough and fair. Rowland requested this inquiry after a white police officer in Hartford killed a fourteen year old black teenager. Pete advised me that the news media would be covering the meeting. He would, he told me, be there for support.

I agreed to speak at the council meeting. I didn't do it because Pete or the Commissioner asked me to. I needed to do it for myself. I wanted the council and anyone else who would listen to understand how the shootings had affected both me and my family. I also wanted to deliver my opinion on the way my department had handled both situations, which is to say badly.

On October 15th I met Pete Curley at the Law Enforcement

Council Meeting in Rocky Hill and spoke to the council. When I arrived I was shocked at the abundance of media coverage. All three major TV networks were present, as well as a number of reporters from area newspapers. Their presence made me extremely nervous. I hated talking in front of people in general, but talking to strangers about such personal feelings in such an open forum, made me sick. To have it televised made it even more nauseating. When I am in uniform I can hide behind the authority persona the uniform and badge provide, and I can talk to people without any fear or nervousness. But when I am in civilian clothing, which I was that day, that protection is gone.

When I began talking about the first shooting a tidal wave of pain and sorrow erupted inside of me. As I described the scene of the shooting in graphic detail I felt myself begin to cry. I remember thinking to myself great, I'm fucking crying on TV and my wife, mother, father, sisters, friends and co-workers are watching and they are all going to think that I am a giant pussy. What serial killer cries on TV (love ya, Jeff). I'm too tough for this, or at least I should be. As my eyes welled up with tears, but before they began rolling uncontrollably down my face, I asked the commission for a short break. Pete escorted me outside and asked me if I wanted to stop speaking. I told him I would go on, and after a few minutes I composed myself and returned to the podium. I told the panel that I felt penalized for doing my job because the investigations were too lengthy and I had been placed on desk duty during the first investigation. I told them that desk duty was a punishment and was more stressful than being involved in the shootings. I also asserted that police officers who were involved in shootings should receive mandatory counseling and that the agency should cover all the associated costs. I told the commission that I had paid for the counseling I received after the shootings out of my own pocket.

After the council meeting I drove home thinking I didn't have to worry about the news media putting me on television or in the paper because there were so many other officers speaking. But that wasn't the case. By the time I arrived home my sister had called my wife and mother and told them that I was crying on TV and all this other bullshit. Of course I had to deal with it when I got home. What's wrong, they wanted to know. What can we do for you? I just wanted it to all go away. I said what I had to say in front of the council and whatever happened there happened. I was done with it. The next day there was a picture of me in the newspaper crying. Whatever.

Bob Child / Associated Press

Chapter 15

Shots were fired

In late April 2001 a very good friend and co-worker, Don Frederick, was involved in a motorcycle accident in the town where I grew up and still reside. Oddly enough, he crashed his motorcycle at the bottom of the hill where I live. He survived the crash only to die a few days later at Hartford Hospital from his injuries. The only saving grace was that Don lived long enough for his family, close friends and co-workers to say goodbye to him. Seeing him lying there in the hospital bed with an alien-sized head, asleep, was not how I wanted to remember him. That was a tough moment for me. Don had many close friends at Troop E, and we were able to support one another through those tough times. I was glad to have worked with him, and more importantly, to have been friends with him.

I soon learned from the Attorney General's Office of the State of Connecticut my trial for civil rights violations was going to start in late summer 2001. During the summer everyone who was at the shooting scene met with State's Attorney Steve Sarnowski to explain what they had seen the night of the shooting. During the meeting, one of the troopers from traffic explained that he had shown up just as I was firing the last shot and stated that he would have shot Parsons if I hadn't. We all looked at him, including the attorney, and asked him what the hell he was talking about. Everyone knew that the only people present at the scene during the shooting were Stowell, Kerry and me, and no one could understand why our colleague was basically lying to make himself seem more heroic. But this behavior is nothing new in our department. Instead of acknowledging someone who has done something positive, many troopers will try to jump on the bandwagon. This is self-manipulation and masturbation at its best. State's Attorney Sarnowski advised the trooper that as long as he told the jury what he had actually seen, and not what he wanted to see, the defense attorney would have a hard time tripping him up during examination. Good advice.

During the meeting Attorney Sarnowski had me listen to the tape of Troop E's radio transmissions from that night in order to identify, by name, the individuals on the tape. When I listened to it for the first time in his office I got chills. I heard the excitement and the fear in every-one's voices as the chaos unfolded. I could hear the fear in the voice of the 911 caller, Lee Yaworski, who was yelling to his brother-in-law, off-duty police officer Michael Suprenant, from the payphone outside of McDonald's, that Parsons had a gun. I heard the anxiety in my voice when I told Stowell to block Parsons' vehicle as he attempted to flee behind McDonald's. I heard the female employee and the customers inside McDonald's screaming into the phone to the desk trooper as shots were fired. I heard the desk trooper frantically advising respond-ing troopers that shots were fired. And I heard the unmistakable fear and disbelief in my voice when I yelled for the desk troopers to send a supervisor and EMS to the scene because the suspect was down with one shot to the head. I still get goose bumps reading this.

I requested a copy of the radio transmission in order to prepare for my testimony at trial. In the back of my mind, however, I just wanted a copy of it. Part of me wanted it because it would be cool to have, and part of me wanted it to keep what happened fresh in my mind. Listen-ing to the tape once or twice a week would get my blood pumping and would give me an edge, almost like the first shooting had. It was an added crutch. Whenever I felt disinterested in my work I would listen to the tape and snap back into Robocop mode. In some small way I thought it would also help me get over what I had been through and what I had done.

I listened to the tape during a therapy session, and then discussed it with my shrink, Dr. Hall. I still have the tape, but I haven't listened to it for years. I am curious how I would react if I listened to it now. Proba-bly the hairs on my arms would still stand up and I would get that same anxious feeling I always felt when I listened to it in my car, alone.

I had asked my wife to listen to it once, but she had no interest in hearing it. I think deep down she was afraid to hear fear in my voice. If she did she might not have allowed me to continue to be a police officer. Over the years she has heard stories about how I handle myself in dan-gerous and stressful situations, and I am sure she didn't want to believe that even I might be vulnerable in certain situations. It's probably best all-around if she never has to hear that truth.

Chapter 16

Isn't it true...?

On one of the most devastating days in U.S. history, September 11, 2001, I was in a Federal Court House in New Haven picking a jury for my trial on civil rights violations. Not long into the process, the female judge, who I figured to be in her eighties, walked into the courtroom, advised us that two small planes had hit the World Trade Center, and dismissed us. Prior to leaving the courthouse, I called my wife and learned that our country was under attack. As I was driving home listening to the radio, I learned that another plane struck the Pentagon and fighter jets were scrambling toward a fourth plane possibly heading for the White House. At this point I was freaking out because my sister Maureen lived right outside of Washington DC, in Virginia, and was a police officer there. I had no idea what danger this invasion would put her in.

I called into work and was told that the government authorities were planning to use the Metro North and Amtrak trains as a sort of moving mortuary and that everyone in the Criminal Investigations Units within the Connecticut State Police was being sent to the train station in Norwalk to remove the dead bodies from the WTC site from the trains. In the span of two hours I was in Federal Court, at home watching the footage of the planes hitting the Twin Towers, kissing my wife, daughter and recently born infant son goodbye, and then driving to work to remove what I imagined would be thousands of dead bodies from a train. As we all soon learned, there were not any bodies to remove. Even the body parts were too small to collect.

The following day I headed back to Federal Court as my fellow police officers from the state were heading to New York in droves to assist the NYPD and NYFD with finding their comrades. It sickened me not to be with them.

As I was driving across the bridge on I-95 that spans the Connecticut River between Old Lyme and Old Saybrook, on the morning of September 12th, I found myself stuck in south bound traffic heading toward New York. A pick-up truck with three firemen pulled up next to me and asked if I could give them an escort toward the city. A large

American flag was blowing in the back of the bed of their truck and they had written USA in large letters all over the body. I put on my lights and sirens and escorted them as far as New Haven in the break down lane, the whole time thinking of saying "fuck it" and escorting them all the way to the city so I wouldn't have to deal with this bullshit trial. I knew that my buddy Stowell was on his way there with his cadaver dog, along with the rest of the Connecticut State Police K-9 Unit. I was jealous of them all, and am still resentful that I wasn't able to be a responder to 9/11, all because of the bogus trial.

My family, friends and coworkers frequently told me that what I had done in the line of duty was heroic, but that is not how I look at it. I had done my job in difficult situations during extraordinary circumstances. That's it. However, I believe that any person who helped in any small way at the WTC is a HERO! Stowell is a HERO! I would have much rather been sifting through the torn remains of the victims of the 9/11 tragedy with him, in hopes of finding survivors, than sitting in a courtroom dealing with such nonsense. At Ground Zero I would have been serving a purpose.

I reluctantly turned my vehicle off the highway and returned to the Federal Courthouse in New Haven that Wednesday morning. Prior to the start of the trial, my parents and wife expressed interest in attending court to support me. Not wanting them to hear any of the gruesome details of the case, or to see any of the gory photos, I asked them not to come. My mother was beside herself, which I could understand. But I needed to do this myself. I had survived this long doing things my way and I didn't want to change things then. I didn't want my parents to see me getting beat up by Attorney Williams while I was on the stand, and I sure as hell didn't want them to see me get upset or cry if my emotions ran high. In making the choice whether to have them there or not, I would picture myself being cross-examined by that "waste of skin" while watching my wife or my parents break down in the court room. I knew I couldn't handle that. Dealing with an armed felon would be easier for me then seeing my loved ones upset. The job is business, not personal. My mother thought that I didn't want her there, but that was not the case. I wanted to protect her.

The trial was quite the experience. Being on trial significantly deepened my depression. On top of that, the events in our country that unfolded over the course of the next few weeks added greatly to my misery. I began, more than ever, to hate any current or former criminal defense attorney. To me they are the scum of the earth. They are actually the dirt below the pile of dog shit that a car salesman stepped in. Joseph Parsons Senior, father of the late Joseph Parsons, had retained the devil himself, Civil Rights Attorney John R. Williams. The same John R. Williams who, as I have mentioned, represented the black Panthers in the 1960's in this fine liberal state of Connecticut. Just saying his name makes me crazy. He is the only person I've ever wanted to kill in my life. I would run him over with my car if he was walking in a crosswalk. I would throw gasoline on him if he was on fire. I would rip his eyes out through his asshole if he was standing in front of me. That's how much hatred I have for this man. Not only did he take a $10,000 retainer fee from poor Mr. Parsons, but he didn't even have the decency to be present during jury selection. His subordinates, to whom he entrusted this crucial part of the trial, were so incompetent that they picked a supervisor from the State of Connecticut Department of Corrections and a former ten-year employee of the Connecticut State Police. The ex-trooper was chosen as the jury foreman by the other jurors. If he were really acting in the best interest of his client, Attorney Williams would have declined to take the case because he had no chance in hell of winning it.

For those unfamiliar with the history of The Black Panther Party, they existed between the mid-1960s through the mid-1970s to promote Black Power. It was started by Bobby Seale and Huey P. Newton in 1966 in California and became very big in US politics as a significant social, political and cultural movement. The early goals of the Party were to protect African American neighborhoods from police brutality, but that changed over the course of time and they became more involved in socialist and communist doctrines designed to foster benefits for all of the country's under-privileged. But regardless of their philosophies, they crossed the line. Always a very militant and provocative group, some of the group members grew too big for their britches.

On May 21, 1969, actually probably right around the time my parents were getting that twinkle in their eye, a Black Panther member, Alex Rackley, then nineteen years old, was brought to the New Haven office of the Panthers, on suspicion of being an FBI informant. After two days of torture he confessed, at which point he was taken to Middlefield and shot twice, once in the head by Warren Kimbro, and once in the chest by Lonnie McLucas. National Panther "Field Marshal" George Sams Jr. was also present. They threw his body into the Coginchaug River. In all, nine Panthers were arrested in connection with the murder; the infamous "New Haven 9". McLucas confessed, and Kimbro and Sams became informants. These were the people Attorney Williams had represented. Now he was out to nail me.

I wore my uniform throughout the course of the trial, which lasted a week, on the advice of my attorney. He wanted the jury to see me as a police officer to underscore the uniqueness of my job and the danger involved. He wanted them to see me in uniform as the dead guy did the night I shot him. He also believed that the jury would have more sympathy for me if I was dressed in uniform. The courtroom was large and empty and except for the judge, jury, the attorneys, Mr. Parsons, the stenographer and me, the only person in the room was Wendy. I felt like I was in one of those medical TV shows having surgery with a few doctors and nurses in the room and all the medical students, like the jury, watching the surgery from up above me in a glass-walled room.

While Stowell was off in the service of our country at the WTC, I was relegated to hearing myself portrayed as the monster in the gray shirt with the blue epaulet. The trial began with opening statements from both attorneys. My attorney, Steve Sarnowski, explained to the jurors that I was acting in self-defense the night I shot Joseph Parsons. Parsons was a violent felon with significant substance and alcohol problems who had pointed a gun at my head. As I suspected, Attorney Williams told the jury that the death of Joseph Parsons was a result of my overly aggressive behavior and that I had a history of this type of conduct throughout my career. Obviously Attorney Williams was referring to my first shooting because no one had ever filed a complaint about me for police brutality. He continued to give further details about how Joseph Parsons was a lost soul with a shitty upbringing and how he had developed a drinking problem as a result. He adamantly pointed out to the jury that I was the one to be blamed for Parsons' death; Parsons was the innocent victim. It was extremely hard for me to sit there and listen to Williams tell deliberate lie after lie about me and what had happened that night. But I had promised Steve, at our first meeting years previously, that I would sit straight up in my chair and keep my hands folded on my lap during my trial. He told me that the judge and the jury would be watching me like a hawk to see my reactions. He knew what

I'd be feeling and how I'd want to react; in any different setting I would have stood up and defended myself against the sensational lies Attorney Williams was spewing in the courtroom. But I was good and somehow I managed to sit quietly next to my attorney, hands folded, gaze strong. In reality I wanted to wring Attorney Williams' neck.

Attorney Williams, true to form, did his best to get me riled.

"Isn't it true, Trooper Patterson, that this is not the first time you've murdered someone?"

"Objection, Your Honor," my lawyer shouted, jumping to his feet. The judge ordered the prosecuting attorney to halt his line of questioning, and called both lawyers to the bench. The jury was directed to leave the courtroom.

As this activity went on, I was sitting in the witness box, my state trooper's hat in my lap, my uniform thick against my body, my feet glued to the wooden floor. I tried to listen to what the judge and lawyers were saying, but my head felt heavy and it fell forward until all I could see was my own reflection in the spit-shined black leather of my boots. A drop of moisture struck the floor, and I realized I was weeping.

I was trapped in the witness chair, physically, mentally, and emotionally. I was here because I was being sued by the father of Joseph Parsons, whom I had killed in the line of duty on December 27, 1998. The elder Parson's attorney was none other than the formidable civil rights lawyer John R. Williams, who made a name for himself representing Black Panther Party members in the 1960s.

Today, Williams had directly disobeyed the judge's orders, and brought up a previous shooting I had been involved in. Murder, as he called it. I had been on the Connecticut State Police force for fewer than six years, and had shot and killed two armed men in the line of duty. Justified shootings, in the eyes of the law, but I was the one on trial, accused of murder not once, but twice. Despite all I had gone through since I joined the force, all the danger and witnessed trauma, this was the lowest point in my life. I felt alone, trapped on the witness stand while my future was debated a few feet away. I felt vulnerable, certain that everyone in the courtroom could see that, as well as the tears that rolled down my cheek. In that moment, I did not feel like a man.

I looked to my wife Wendy, sitting in the front row of the otherwise empty courtroom. It seemed as if she were miles, not merely yards, away. The pain of being alone was nearly unbearable, but I could see the anger on her face, and the looks of sympathy and support she gave me. That helped, and I willed myself to suck it up and take whatever was dealt me.

Parsons' father had sued me for denying him his civil liberties by depriving him of his right and ability to have a relationship with his son. When I had first learned of the lawsuit I couldn't believe that the courts would actually entertain such a laughable idea. What a crock of shit, had been my exact thought. Now, I was on the stand being called a two-time murderer by a powerful, well-known attorney who advertises that he specializes in cases involving police brutality.

It struck me as ironic that Joseph Parsons Senior was able to sue me for killing his son in self-defense, but I was unable to sue him for raising a son who fucked up my life through his own violent actions. My thoughts grew darker, imagining that I'd sue Parsons for even having a son, for not aborting him, for being an asshole of a father...but then the judge sustained the objection, and the trial resumed, and I did my best to represent my profession, but more importantly, my family.

Ever since I was a young boy I had wanted to be a police officer. It was in my blood. Both my grandfathers, John F. Bowen and Vere L. Patterson were Hartford Connecticut Police Officers in the 1950s and 1960s. My uncle, John F. Bowen II, retired as a captain with the Hartford Police Department and two of my first cousins, Captain Joseph Buyak, and Lieutenant James Buyak are still employed by the Hartford Police Department. Their sister, Laura Buyak, recently retired from the department as a detective. I also have second and third cousins who are either retired police officers or employed in other departments in the state.

I became a Connecticut State Trooper in 1992, despite my mother, Bonnie Bowen Patterson, begging me not to. As the daughter of a police officer she knew firsthand how dangerous a cop's life was and how the work negatively affects the lives of spouses and children. Much to her dismay, my sister Maureen Patterson Mckeon also followed in our family's tradition and became a Fairfax County Virginia Police Officer in 1999.

I had always wanted to follow in the footsteps of my grandfathers. But there was a hiring freeze in Hartford during the late 1980s into the early 1990s, so I attended the University of Connecticut and studied sociology. When the hiring freeze ended, I applied to the Connecticut State Police. My family questioned me about why I wanted to become a State Trooper or "Big Hat" as the city cops like to call us. They thought that working in the boondocks of eastern Connecticut would be less dangerous and easier than working in an urban setting. My response to them was that a city cop's back-up is fewer than two minutes away, while a Trooper's back-up could take a half hour to arrive; so therefore you have to be tougher to be a Trooper than a city cop. At the time, it was a joke, friendly family teasing. Today, I wasn't laughing.

In my eyes a cop is a cop is a cop. There is no difference between a Hartford Police Officer, a Fairfax County Police Officer, a Connecticut State Trooper or a sheriff in a town of one hundred people. On any given day one of us could make the ultimate sacrifice and lay down our own life in order to save the life of another human being. Or, be called upon to make a life or death decision that results in another life being laid down.

I became a cop in 1992 at the ripe old age of twenty-two and by the time I was twenty-eight I had killed two armed felons in separate, justified incidents. I sustained numerous physical injuries over the years (broken wrist, sprained ankles, torn ligaments), and have had multiple surgeries on my thumb and both shoulders related to on-the-job injuries.

None of that compares to the mental injuries I have suffered. By the age of thirty I had developed Post Traumatic Stress Disorder (PTSD). Depression was tearing my life apart. Police work is 99% boredom and 1% sheer terror. It's that one percent that attacks your soul and rips it apart. Colonel Trautman said in First Blood, "Rambo has eaten things that would make a billy goat puke." Well, I've seen things that would make a billy goat puke—things that have changed my entire being. For what I have done, I hope my children will forgive me; if forgiveness is needed. For what I have become, I will certainly need their forgiveness.

During the first days, the only time I questioned whether or not we were going to win or lose the trial was when the trooper from the Connecticut State Police Traffic Division testified on my behalf, and sounded instead like he was working on behalf of Attorney Williams. Against the advice of Attorney Sarnowski he perjured himself on the stand and ended up looking like a complete jackass. He had shown up on the scene after the shooting, but claimed to have seen me shoot the perp, stating he was going to shoot the guy himself if I hadn't. While he was testifying, my attorney and I looked at each other in disbelief, puzzled as to what was going on. Luckily, in the end, his testimony had no bearing on the case.

When it came time to call Stowell to the witness stand, my attorney explained to the judge and jury that Stowell was at Ground Zero with his cadaver dog searching for survivors (at that point there was still hope there might be someone alive in the rubble) and requested that the statement Stowell provided the night of the shooting be used in lieu of actual court testimony. This was not acceptable to Attorney Williams. He seemed convinced that Stowell was hiding something, and he wanted the opportunity to cross-examine him. The fact that Stowell was at Ground Zero doing God's work wasn't a good enough excuse for him. For a period of time the judge considered having the Connecticut State Police helicopter fly down to New York, pick up Stowell, fly him back for an hour of testimony and then fly him back to the city. After several hours of consideration, the judge sided with my attorney and used Stowell's statement. You can't make this shit up.

On the third day of the trial it was my turn to testify. As soon as I sat in the witness chair my sergeant, John Rich, and Detectives Steve Rief and Ted Parker walked into the courtroom and sat down next to Wendy. Perfect timing, right? Not for me. It made me more nervous. I loved all those guys and I was glad they were there to support Wendy, but I became more anxious, not wanting to look bad in front of them.

Initially I thought my testimony went smoothly. I didn't have any problem staying on task, answering the questions I was asked, or looking at the judge and jury while providing my answers. I had testified before in serious felony cases and each time I became more comfortable on the stand. But my sense of well-being was short lived. Williams had started out with basic questions concerning my education and academy police training. Then he immediately switched gears and started talking about my "complaint-filled history" as a police officer. Knowing full well that only one person had ever made a complaint against me, I stayed firm with my answers and rode out the first big wave. Then came the zinger that totally caught me off guard—he accused me of murdering someone before.

With the jury out of the courtroom, the judge admonished Attorney Williams and told him not to bring up my previous shooting again, and that if he did, he would be disbarred indefinitely. The Bailiff brought the jury back into the courtroom and returned them to the jury box. The judge advised them to disregard the last statements made by Attorney Williams.

Williams resumed his questioning by stating, "Trooper Patterson, isn't it true that two years ago you killed another person?" Again Steve jumped up and yelled "Objection", but the Judge was already verbally raking Williams over the coals.

Now I was fucking fuming. I stared at Williams like I had Superman's laser vision and could burn a hole through him and send him into Hell. I knew the Judge wasn't going to hold him accountable in any way and that this asshole wasn't going to be disbarred. I figured I would have to sit there and take it in the tail pipe like every other person he'd tried to fuck in the past. But I knew that he knew I had won the case before he even took it and that this was his one shot to piss me off to the point that I would become angry and turn into a raving lunatic on the stand in order to prove that I was a crazy homicidal cop that killed people for pleasure. But I was good and sat quietly.

I won the case. On the last day of the trial, after the jury acquitted me of any wrong doing, Attorney Williams (dick smack, to me) had the audacity to congratulate me. As I moved toward him to rip his face off, Wendy grabbed my hand and not so gently led me away.

Chapter 17

The tattoo

Interview by Deborah L. Mandel
with Wendy and John Patterson

I have known John Patterson for over thirty years. I have watched him grow from a gangly youth into a responsible, mature, and dedicated police officer, husband and father. A few weeks after the first shooting, we went on vacation together, and I had the opportunity to talk with him. He asked me if there was something wrong with the fact that the shooting didn't bother him. I suggested that it might take some time to settle in. It worried me, however, that he felt nothing at all. I wondered if this emotional numbness was a reflection of John's innate personality—his tough guy demeanor—or if the feelings had gone deeply underground and would come to haunt him at some later time. But for John, having been put in the position of taking a life in the line of duty, it was just another day on the job.

When the second shooting occurred, I became fearful for John's well-being. He was now married and recently had become a father. I knew he was a resilient and controlled individual, but even an ironman can be felled by such trauma. As you have read in John's description of the events, the trauma hit, and it hit hard. I was relieved when John told me that he had acknowledged the effect of the shootings and had begun psychotherapy. Recently John told me that as part of his continued healing and well-being, and to alert other officers to the inherent psychological risks associated with their profession, he was writing a book about his experiences and his personal battle with Post Traumatic Stress Disorder (PTSD). He asked me to help him edit his book, interview some of the important people in his life, and describe how they saw the impact of the shootings on him. I told him it would be an honor.

November 2011. John and Wendy join my husband Jim and me for dinner to discuss how the book is progressing. John is eight months out from retirement. His and Wendy's marriage has not only survived his twenty years on the force, but has thrived. They are as close today, if not more, as when they met when Wendy was in High School running track. Wendy is the steadying force behind John. She does not let him sit and wallow in his pain. She prods and pushes and reminds him when it is time to get back into therapy because he is sinking into depression. She manages the household and worries that if she ever goes back to work, their marriage would fall apart without her there 24/7. She continually pushes him to communicate.

It hasn't been easy. When John came home from work in a mood, Wendy would have no idea if it was something about work or about her. At first, John wouldn't discuss his day with Wendy, which was his way of protecting her. But it was extremely lonely and frustrating for her when he was so quiet and withdrawn. There were long periods of time when John would come home from work and nap for several hours. She felt like she had four children instead of a husband and three kids. And despite how much she liked and loved him, sometimes, as Wendy told me, "I just wanted to kill him."

Finally, once John had established his therapeutic relationship with Dr. Hall, Wendy joined him for some sessions. Dr. Hall was able to give them both the coping skills they needed. Wendy learned that she had to ask John how his day went and whether he was quiet and subdued because of his work or because of her. Mostly, John had to talk to her about his experiences. Dr. Hall assured him that Wendy was tough enough to hear what was going on.

As a result, John began calling Wendy and telling her a little of what happened at work, allowing Wendy time to prepare for his return home at the end of his shift. For example, Wendy recounted one incident in which John had called her, upset because he was investigating a serious sexual assault. The victim was similar in age and appearance to his mother Bonnie. Wendy could tell over the phone that it upset John greatly. Although she was sad for him, she was glad that John called her instead of trying to deal with it on his own. It helped Wendy enormously to know what was going on in John's world so she could respond to him accordingly. Wendy thanked Dr. Hall for this positive change. Understanding that his feelings were not about her shifted Wendy's ability to feel good about herself and their marriage, enabling her to help John in the ways he needed. She would constantly remind him that he had three beautiful children, a wonderful wife, a great house, and to start paying more attention to them and get out of his funk. Unfortunately, stepping away from PTSD is not that easy.

Wendy is as vivacious as John is sullen. Without her, it is hard to imagine how John would have survived these last years, yet I believe that she could not survive without him either. He is the love of her life and as she said during our evening together, "I believe everything happens for a reason."

Wendy's life has not always been an easy one. She had her personal issues growing up, and then tragically, when she was twenty-one, her younger brother died in a car accident. She is not a stranger to pain. Despite all she survived in her lifetime, she never could have imagined the dramatic, and traumatic, turns her life would take when she became engaged to John. To this day she mourns the loss of her 'Johnny' and would like nothing better than to have him back. She is dealing with her own vicarious traumatization, the secondary impact on her of having her husband involved in life and death traumatic events. From John's perspective, she like him, has begun to hate people. She is quick to tell John to "pull that asshole over" when they are on the road, and she no longer has the same tolerance she used to for nasty or intolerant people. Her world view has changed right along with John's.

Life in the Patterson household is normal, yet completely abnormal. John goes to work. He coaches his son's football and baseball teams. But he needs to have his eyes on his children all of the time. Every few minutes, according to Wendy, he will go upstairs to see where they are, if they are okay, and she will have to remind him to calm down. On the other hand, he had his children watch Restrepo, a documentary about the Afghanistan war, to begin to desensitize them to the reality of the world. The children do not know about the shootings, but are coming close to an age where they will need to be told, before a schoolmate taunts them one day about their daddy the killer.

The images of the shootings and of the many critical incidents he has witnessed are permanently tattooed on John's brain. In addition to the shootings, he feels he had a hand in the death of three others during his career. He feels responsible for two individuals who committed suicide shortly after he interviewed them in the April Pennington homicide investigation, and one other man who committed suicide shortly after John arrested him. In this situation, John had followed up on a complaint by two teenage girls who described an older, fat, white guy who would be waiting for them at their bus stop a few days a week. He would sit in his car watching them as they got off the bus. A few times he followed them slowly in his car, to their house. One time they ended up walking by him and he was masturbating. The girls were able to provide a description of the car and a background check determined that he had been doing the same thing to girls in Norwich the previous year.

A few days later, John found the man sitting in the spot the girls described. He tried to drive away, and when John stopped him his pants were undone. John questioned him and because "he was such a cock, no pun intended", John arrested him for interfering with a police officer. The girls positively identified the perpetrator. A month later the man's neighbors called the Troop because of a foul smell coming from his apartment. He had shot himself in the head shortly after his arrest, but prior to killing himself he had sprinkled foot powder all over his apartment, inches thick, to mask the smell of his decaying body. He had actually melted into his chair. John is convinced the man thought he would be the one to find the decaying body and that he did it to fuck with him. Luckily he was in class that day, and laughed when the sergeant called to let him know, because he didn't have to be there.

All these pictures and feelings are too much for any one man to bear. John wants them out. He imagines that if he could get the images out of his brain and onto another part of his body he would no longer be in as much pain. His idea was to put the deepest most disturbing images of how he feels into a tattoo. He first asked his friend George Leitkowski, a police sketch artist to design a tattoo of the image he carries inside his head.

This drawing depicts John as the grim reaper, scythe in his right hand, and the Scales of Justice in his left.

The second design, created by professional artist Timothy Boor, and the one John wants to use, is by far one of the most haunting images I have ever seen.

For John, having someone see the emotional weight of what he is carrying internally will be cathartic. While he feels okay right now, no one, he says, can understand what it is like to cause the death of somebody if they haven't killed someone themselves; an experience that leaves him feeling alone and often depressed. Jay understands, a few other guys from his old group understand, but Wendy never really can, nor can anyone else who has not gone through the experience themselves. "It doesn't matter that they were in the wrong and that I had to shoot. What matters is that I took the life of another. It is impossible to let go of that."

John wants this tattoo on his calf. Wendy vehemently opposes it. For her the tattoo is a reminder that she cannot fix him, that he is broken. It saddens her that this is the way he thinks and feels inside. In order for her to continue to support John through the years, she has had to distance herself from the grisly details. The picture of the tattoo brought her face to face with John's demons, his unyielding pain-filled reality. In hindsight, she wishes she had never seen it.

Wendy is concerned about the impact of the tattoo on their children, who still do not know the details about his two shootings. She is afraid it will traumatize them to see the image. It troubles her that when John is coaching football it will be visible to all the children, parents and grandparents watching the games, as he always wears shorts on the field. How they will view him then? Can he remain just another dad coaching his son? But she is also quick to say that if John is sure it will help him to heal, he should get it. John's current concession (and he is taking his time making up his mind) is that he would put it on the side of his thigh, so it would not be visible to the public. Wendy's remaining concern is how it will affect her; seeing that image anywhere on his body will haunt her.

When John talks about the tattoo, he is clear it is not the actual shootings that haunt him; once they were over—they were over. Rather it is the images of Jay's blood curdling screams—Joe, Joe, Joe—and the worry that if he hadn't gotten to Parsons before Stowell and Blizzard, that Stowell would be dead, which he believes would have destroyed him for life. These are the images and thoughts that are impossible for him to shake. Once the images are there, they are always there, they become part of you; a part that can never be erased. They are permanently etched in his brain and he wants them transformed into a tattoo.

It is the only way, he believes, to show others how he feels on the inside, to show how he has been branded by his PTSD

Spending time with Wendy and John is always a pleasure. They are an endearing couple, as loving and full of compassion as any two people we know. But they certainly have had to scale mountains to be where they are today. Jim perfectly summed up our evening's conversation: Wendy, takes care of everybody in the family, while John takes care of everybody else; a modern day Atlas, holding the entire world on his shoulders.

Chapter 18

Brian and Sach

Over the course of the next few years there were two events that greatly impacted me. The most grievous involved the death of a five year old boy, Brian Brown, who died at the hands of his father, Paul Brown. Trooper Chris Sottile was patrolling the town of Griswold on the evening shift on the 8th of February 2002, when he was stopped by Patricia Brown, Brian's mother, who was frantically searching for her son. She had custody of Brian, but she'd allowed his father, Paul, to pick Brian up at school the day before and to sleep over his father's house, with the understanding that Paul would drive Brian to school the following morning. But when Brian hadn't shown up at school and Paul didn't show up at court for their scheduled divorce hearing earlier in the day, Patricia reported Brian missing. Prior to that she had driven to Paul's house and found his car hidden behind the house, but no one appeared to be home. After notifying Troop E of the situation, Trooper Sottile followed Patricia to the house and tried to make contact with Brown. When they arrived at the home there were lights on, and as Sottile was knocking on the front door, Patricia yelled that there was someone in the driveway.

As Sottile walked toward the driveway he noticed a white male leaning on a red pick-up truck parked in the driveway. The man was dazed and confused and appeared to be intoxicated. Patricia identified him as her husband, Paul Brown. Sottile escorted Brown back to the front of the house to speak with him. Brown was evasive and refused to give him his full name. He threw up on himself numerous times while sitting on the front steps. Sottile returned to the red pick-up to look for any signs of Brian. While checking the immediate area surrounding the truck, Sottile found a pistol grip shotgun lying on the ground behind the truck. Sottile immediately returned to the front of the house and placed Brown in handcuffs for safety purposes. When he searched him, Sottile found a large folding pocket knife, a smaller pocket knife, a 12 gauge 00 buck shotgun shell, keys, a handcuff key on a key chain in his pockets and a handcuff key on a necklace around his neck.

As Sottile unloaded the shotgun to secure it in his vehicle, he noticed there was one shell in the chamber and four rounds in the tube. After updating Troop E, Sottile returned to Paul and asked him where Brian was. Paul told Sottile that Brian was with Paul's mother, but refused to provide her phone number. Sottile located the phone number in Paul's cell phone and contacted Brian's grandmother, who told him that she didn't have Brian and hadn't seen either Brian or Paul in a week.

A short time later Trooper First Class French arrived at the house and began a search of the area for Brian. When he couldn't locate the boy, he went to speak with Paul's neighbors. Meanwhile Trooper First Class O'Donnell arrived with his K-9 and searched the residence for Brian, also with negative results. As the troopers continued to ask Brown about the whereabouts of his son, Trooper First Class Fabian arrived with Paul's parents and brother. It was Fabian's hope that Paul would tell family members where Brian was. But he didn't. Trooper Fabian, looking more closely at the secured pistol grip shotgun, observed what he believed to be body tissue and blood splatter on the barrel.

Sergeant Hassett arrived next at the scene. He searched the area surrounding Brown's home, using his flashlight to look into the interior of a Dodge Intrepid that was hidden behind the house. On the front seat he observed two sets of handcuffs, two hunting knives, a set of keys and a strand of twine. In the back seat there were blankets, a child safety seat and a box of 12 gauge (00 buck) shotgun shells. When he examined the bed of the truck, Sergeant Hassett saw what he believed to be blood on the tool box attached to the inside of the bed as well as a blood-like smear on the lower portion of the driver's door. Trooper First Class O'Donnell and Sergeant Hassett used a crow bar to open the locked tool box in hopes of finding an injured Brian Brown, not a dead one. Sadly, what they found was an object, the length of the tool box, covered in a green wool blanket. As they pulled back a corner of the blanket, they exposed a small foot inside of a sneaker and a leg clothed in blue jeans. A stuffed animal lay on the boy's torso. When Sergeant Hassett lifted the opposite corner of the wool blanket, they saw massive trauma to the boy's head. The corpse was a white male, who fit the approximate age and size of missing five year old Brian. He had what appeared to be a gunshot wound to his head. In reality there was nothing left of his head. Brian's shoulders were still there, and maybe a small piece of his neck, but not much else.

After the discovery of Brian Brown's body, I was contacted by my sergeant, John Rich, and asked to respond to the scene with my fellow detectives and assist with the investigation, which lasted all night and well into the next day. Our investigation revealed that Paul Brown had shot his son in the head with a shotgun at the Patchaug Rod and Gun Club. A search of the grounds there revealed that the brutal murder had taken place in the middle of a dirt road near the entrance to the facility. A large amount of blood, as well as pieces of human skull were located on the dirt roadway.

When detectives brought Paul Brown to the Jewett City Resident Trooper's Office to interview him, they discovered a large amount of blood on his blue jeans. After refusing to cooperate with detectives, Brown was arrested for Capital Felony Murder in the death of his son, Brian Brown. Brown was later convicted on this charge and sentenced to life in prison without the possibility of parole.

When it came time to process the scene, including taking photographs and collecting evidence, I was ill prepared for what I saw. In my career, I had seen numerous dead bodies, but they were mostly adults, and all those years I had made light of the situations. As I've said before, my fellow detectives and I were famous for cracking jokes and doing stupid things at a scene to make people laugh in order to help deal with the trauma. I would remove myself mentally from the scene and act like what I was witnessing wasn't real. I would put myself into a vacuum where the dead person was road kill or a piece of meat at the butcher shop. That's how I dealt with dead people, and the way I believe most cops deal with the shock and horror of seeing another dead human being. If we pretended that what we were witnessing wasn't real, then it didn't happen. So we did things and said things to make it a little less true in our minds. This event changed all of that.

When it came time to remove Brian Brown from inside of the tool box, all of the detectives looked at each other like, "hey, I'm not going to touch that fucking blanket." At this point most of us were sick to our stomachs because the lid to the tool box had been open for quite a while, as photos were being taken of the body.

Then I thought I could sit here and look at the headless horseman's son for the next ten minutes, or I could just get him the fuck out of there. So I climbed up into the pickup truck with another detective, and we each grabbed one end of the green wool blanket, and took Brian out of the box, the whole time staring at his bloodied, lifeless body and that blood soaked stuffed animal his father had put on his stomach. Brian's head looked as if someone had cut out a small hole in a watermelon, placed the barrel of a shotgun inside of it and pulled the trigger. Boom—all gone.

I thought about my daughter Amelia, who at that time was three and a half years old.

As hard as I've tried, I have never forgotten that day. Although I never dreamed about it, or had nightmares because of it, something deep inside of me changed forever. Brian's innocence was taken from him, as was my own. Being at that horrific crime scene changed me as a person; it blackened my soul, weakened my heart and numbed my feelings. Friends often wonder why I hate people so much. How could a father kill his five year old son? It makes me sick to think about it, let alone write about it. Unfortunately, all of the questions I've asked myself over the years, to try to make sense of it, have gone unanswered. I'm sure that's one of the reasons why I'm so fucked up. Evil is inexplicable.

A year later, on January 23rd, 2003, Montville Police Officer Joseph Sachatello (Sach) lost control of his cruiser while responding to a call. He died instantly when his cruiser struck a large tree. It was the coldest night in the history of my life. At the time of the accident a group of coworkers and I were having a few beers in honor of retired Connecticut State Trooper Donald Richardson, who had shot and killed himself a week earlier. Don was a Vietnam Veteran who had worked at Troop E when I started there in January of 1993. He had suffered both psychological and physical wounds during that war, which never left him. After his retirement from the State Police, he had become a Court Marshall at the local courthouse. Don was a drinker and over the years he had trouble dealing with his personal demons left over from the Vietnam conflict. His coworkers told me that Don had a hard time physically getting dressed to go to work every day because of his wounds. But he was a great guy and one of the few veteran troopers who actually talked to me when I started on the job.

We had just arrived at the bar after attending Don's wake when we heard the news about Sach. At first we were told that he had serious injuries and EMS was attempting to cut him out of his cruiser. Periodically we called the barracks to see how things were progressing. Soon a difficult night only became more difficult. While my fellow detectives and I were reminiscing about Don, Sergeant John Rich received the news that Sach had died and that our unit had to process the accident scene. When we arrived, the EMS was still attempting to cut Sach out of his cruiser, which was literally wrapped around the base of the tree. His cruiser had struck the tree in the middle of the driver's door, and the force of the accident was so strong that the driver's seat was completely crushed, leaving it sandwiched against the front passenger side of the vehicle.

A number of Montville Police Officers were also at the scene, waiting for Sach to be removed from his car. I am sure they were there from the beginning, hoping that by some small miracle, he would be pulled from his cruiser alive. But I guess it was his time to go. When Sach was finally freed from the mangled cruiser and placed on a stretcher, and the EMS personnel loaded him into the ambulance, I broke down crying. I hugged my sergeant and cried on his shoulder. Seeing Sach lying dead on that stretcher in full uniform was too much for me to handle. I remember wondering how this could have happened and why. Once again I questioned my faith in God. I tried to rationalize his death in my head, but I never got the answers I was looking for.

For God's sake, I thought, he and his wife just had a baby. Maybe in some small way, I saw myself lying there. If I hadn't shot and killed Joseph Cote and Joseph Parsons, perhaps that would have been me dead on the stretcher. Or maybe I was mourning for yet one more piece of my innocence that had died inside of me. Looking back, that was the worst night of my professional career.

Chapter 19

Interview with Sergeant John Rich
by Deborah L. Mandel
January 2009

"John is a hero of the department. He is not a hero because he had to shoot in the line of duty. He is a hero because he rose to the occasion of taking the necessary steps to deal with the aftermath."
John Rich

O n September 3, 1996, the day John Patterson and Jay Gaughan were dispatched to the home of Michael Cote, John Rich was not working. He had recently been promoted to Sergeant and assigned to Troop E of the Connecticut State Police, the same headquarters where Patterson and Gaughan worked. He recalls breathing a sigh of relief that he did not have to manage the incident, aware of the myriad of issues they would be facing in the wake of their actions.

State Police protocol, in the event of the use of deadly force by a police officer, requires an investigative team lead by a Sergeant from the Major Crime Squad respond to the incident. The shooting site is treated as a crime scene. The Sergeant determines if the officer needs medical attention. Then the officer's duty weapon, his or her uniform, and anything else on their person may be appropriated as evidence.

As soon as an officer uses deadly force, questions begin flooding in. What's going to happen to me? Did I do the right thing? Am I going to get fired? Am I going to be suspended? Am I going to be put on leave and if so, for how long? A giant chasm of great unknowing opens up. The officer is immediately placed on administrative duty while the facts and circumstances of the incident are investigated. The officer is living in limbo while waiting for the outcome of the investigation, which is under the jurisdiction of the State's Attorney's Office in the county in which the incident occurred. At the end of the investigation an opinion is rendered as to whether or not, under state statute, the officer's use of deadly force was justified. Depending on the outcome the officer will be allowed back to his or her job, assigned to a different position, or if the findings are unfavorable, face criminal charges and termination.

Traditionally, there have not been services available for troopers to deal with the emotional consequences of having to use deadly force on the job. If all goes well and they are exonerated of any wrong doing, life goes on as if nothing out of the ordinary had happened. But in fact, something out of the ordinary has happened. Killing another person and facing the threat of being killed oneself can and does frequently cause an emotional backlash, including Post Traumatic Stress Disorder. I interviewed Sergeant John Rich from the Connecticut State Police, John's supervisor after the second shooting incident, about how his department handles these situations in general and about John's experiences in particular.

"Whether a police-involved shooting becomes a more or less traumatic experience for the officer will be determined during the early moments following the situation," Sergeant Rich said when we first spoke in his office at the Ledyard Police Department in October 2008. "It depends on how it is handled initially at the scene, and that depends to a large degree on who is managing it."

Sergeant Rich's ideas on how to manage situations which involve the use of deadly force developed over years of being part of a team that investigated police-involved shootings. To minimize the negative impact of the investigative process, he treats the involved officer with empathy and immediately informs the trooper about what to expect during the investigation.

"I think it is incumbent on us to treat our officers in a tactful way," said Sergeant Rich. "We're not going to give up our investigative responsibilities, but we can do it in such a manner where we don't compromise the investigation but are mindful of what the officer has just been through and how traumatic that can be. We don't want to push too hard. We want to be informative and we want to tell the officer what to expect."

Sergeant Rich initially focuses on gathering basic information regarding the incident. This gives the officer time to process the experience, which in turn leads to a more accurate report of what happened, a better investigation, and a better experience for everyone involved. In Rich's estimation, if you immediately come down on the officer with a barrage of questions, you put that person on the defensive, which will hinder, not further the investigation.

"I can only imagine if it was me in that position," said Sergeant Rich. "The first thing I would want to absorb is that I am okay. I'm safe and I'm okay. My family is safe. That's something that each one of us carries—having people at home to take care of. That would be my first concern. I'm okay and the people at home are okay."

Because of the nature the job, the officer is going to have to provide an accounting of what transpired. But there is a way to obtain better and more accurate information, and that is to be tactful, to not be rushed and to allow the officer time to process. Empathy for the police officer and what he or she has just been through is crucial.

Sergeant Rich's treatment of officers following critical incidents evolved initially because of his personality, and more recently has been refined because of the extensive training he has undertaken. As a supervisor, he realized that he had to learn more about the mental health issues he was seeing in his officers including Post Traumatic Stress Disorder (PTSD), suicide, marital difficulties, alcoholism and other addictions.

"As a supervisor I should have known this stuff. I should have been more cognizant of it. Informally, based on my personality, I knew, but I didn't have any special training on how to actually handle it. There are new protocols in place for handling police involved shootings, inspired in part by John's incidents as well as a few other police involved shootings in New London County, but when John's incidents occurred, there was not much guidance." Rich speaks highly of the State Police, and the changes they are making, but emphasizes that it is important to continue to examine how situations have been handled in the past and how improvements can continue to be made in the present policies.

"I've been close, and had my firearm out numerous times, dozens of times. Things went the right way and people complied," said Sergeant Rich. "They did what I told them to do, and everybody was happy. It went well. It is extraordinary that John was involved in two shootings in such a short period of time as a patrol officer so early in his career. It's just unbelievable." To the best of his knowledge, these circumstances have not happened in the history of the Connecticut State Police, the oldest state police force in the country. Even though he was not part of either investigation, Sergeant Rich recalls that after the second shooting there was some question about where John was going to go in the department. Were they going to put John back out on the streets in a uniform? Would he be in the same type of position? Ultimately the decision was made that John would work under Sergeant Rich in the Major Crime Squad as a sexual assault investigator.

"I remember distinctly, and I am not trying to speak disrespectfully of anyone, that there was a commander in our department who told me in no uncertain terms that John should not be treated any differently than anyone else," said Sergeant Rich, "and that he shouldn't be given this assignment. And my response was—because I've always had a little bit of a problem holding my tongue when I think that something is unjust—have you ever shot and killed anyone in the line of duty?"

"Well no I haven't," the commander replied.

"Then maybe you can make that judgment if you do some day."

Sergeant Rich believed that John deserved to be treated differently than other members of the force because he had already sacrificed enough in the line of duty. In his opinion John earned that special recognition because of what had happened and he knew that if John were assigned to his unit he would make the most of him while he was there.

Sergeant Rich and John talked very little about the shootings during the years that the sergeant supervised him (2001-2005), but he learned enough to know that John had been deeply impacted by what had happened. Rich was aware that John was attending therapy sessions to deal with his PTSD. He was supportive of John going to his weekly sessions, reassuring him that the department would take care of things while he was out of the office. He also told John that he did not need to use his accrued time for the sessions.

"I always felt that in the Major Crime Squad I called them all hours of the night and we didn't give them anything extra. They were doing their job. So I told John, you take care of what you need to take care of. You make sure you're well and your family is well. We'll deal with things as they come."

The years John worked for the Major Crime Squad were during a very difficult period in his life, yet there was never any downturn in John's work performance. He never dropped a step as an investigator and he never lost his passion for doing his job. John's duties involved the investigation of child abuse and child sexual abuse, for which he received extensive training, becoming efficient in dealing with child victims as well as with the perpetrators.

"It was remarkable to me, because he has a little bit of an edge to him," said Sergeant Rich. "He's the life of the party and the class clown. But to see him sit down with those kids and have them draw pictures of what happened to them and watch him work with them, was kind of a paradox. John had an uncanny ability to get things done, in very difficult investigations dealing with child victims. He had a great passion for the job and he was fantastic at it. He set the bar for the guys in our agency."

"When you come right down to it John's a sensitive guy," he continued. "When you see him with the kids, his moral compass is pointed in the right direction. He is a caring individual. And I think that's where a lot of his passion comes from. He will be the one to stand up for a victim and say this is where the abuse stops."

Occasionally Sergeant Rich had to put a leash on John. Let's rethink this, he'd tell him. Let's not rush right in like a bull in a china shop. John's a hard charger, and to this day, he has not slowed down, despite physical injuries to his shoulders which he incurred during the second shooting and other on the job traumas. Even after surgeries to repair his damaged shoulders, Sergeant Rich noticed that there was never a time when John hadn't been moving at 100 miles per hour. "He just goes. He's an unbelievable guy and we had a great working relationship."

"I have a great deal of respect for John, for the way he handled the whole situation," Sergeant Rich said. He admires the courage John showed in dealing with the issues that arose out of his adversities and appreciated his response to dealing with the traumatic aftermath of the two incidents.

"John has this competitive side to him that is unbelievable, almost to the point where he'll take on any fight, sometimes ones I would never advise pursuing. But that is him and that is part of how he's gotten through this."

John's sense of humor stayed strong during this trying time. "One day I'm engaged in a work related conversation on the phone," said Sergeant Rich, "and John appeared in the doorway. He was trying to tell me he had to leave for his appointment and he used sign language, as only John can. He pointed at himself, did a circle around his head, like I'm crazy, and pointed 'I gotta go'. That's just the way it was. There was not a lot of talk about his diagnosis. I knew he had PTSD, and he told me that he was having nightmares and trouble sleeping. I tried to be as supportive as I could in recognizing that and just tried to be a good super to him."

During the time that John worked under Sergeant Rich's supervision, he was sued for wrongful death by the family of the man involved in the second shooting. Sergeant Rich only became aware on the Friday prior to the Monday court date that John's trial was beginning. Rich assumed that there was someone higher up, from a different part of the agency, doing something for John. As it turned out, there was no one.

The magnitude of what it meant for John to go to court did not initially register with Sergeant Rich, but at some point during the first week of the trial, it occurred to him that the department had to do something. One day midweek he told the two detectives working with him that they were going to New Haven to the trial. Sergeant Rich did not ask permission or tell anyone from the department. They just went.

"I remember walking into the court room and there sitting on the front bench alone was Wendy Patterson. That was it. Just Wendy," Sergeant Rich said. "On the other side were the plaintiff and his attorney. I don't think there was anybody else in the courtroom. I remember the look on Wendy's face when we walked in and sat down with her. Court was already in session. I just touched her hand, as a gesture of 'we're here for you', and from the look on her face I know she appreciated it."

Ironically, the day they went was the day the plaintiff's attorney called John to the stand. Rich was impressed at how genuine John sounded as he gave his testimony, despite emotionally struggling at times while he was recounting what happened. When the plaintiff's attorney read sections of the written statement taken after the shooting, John cried. The attorney tried to portray him as a cowboy and a monster. Despite the judge's ruling that John's first shooting not be introduced in any form in this trial because it would be prejudicial, the plaintiff's attorney still attempted to bring it out.

"'Trooper Patterson, this is not the first time you've been...' 'Objection your honor', from John's attorney," recounted Sergeant Rich. "He had to throw it out in front of the jury. Despite the Judge's instructions on the matter, he had to do that. It was absolutely disgraceful and despicable. But I remember thinking that it was okay he was up there; he was going to be alright."

The judge called a recess to discuss the infraction with the two attorneys. When they came back from the Judge's chambers John finished his testimony. Sergeant Rich had no doubt in his mind when he left court that day that the Judge was going to rule in his favor. He went back to the barracks to finish some work. On his way home, driving over the Gold Star Bridge, Sergeant Rich called John and told him that he thought he'd done great and that he was going to be fine. John expressed his appreciation to Rich and the others for coming to court. "There was just something, despite all the business we had to take care of in the office, on-going cases, the day to day business stuff of the Major Crime Squad, just something told me we had to go there that day. And it was the right day."

John was exonerated.

Supervising John gave Sergeant Rich an unusual opportunity for continued contact with an officer dealing with the aftermath of a deadly incident, giving him a deeper understanding of what the process looked like. As an investigator, when he went to a police involved shooting, he only saw a snapshot in time—the moment of the shooting. From his years spent working with John, Sergeant Rich came to understand that the emotional fallout from PTSD never ends. It is—if all goes well—managed. But this only comes about if the officer seeks the help he or she needs.

An officer's mental health in the aftermath of a shooting, or other critical incident, must be dealt with or it can lead to diminished work performance. In the cases that Sergeant Rich has managed it became apparent to him that a problem in the workplace is not due to the officer's lack of caring, or being lazy, but is an indicator that the person needs help. If he sees an officer struggling at work after a traumatic incident, Sergeant Rich will not write him or her up; instead he will help the officer figure out what is happening and direct him or her toward the help he or she needs. He does this quietly and confidentially. Hopefully the officer will take some time off, get things situated, and then come back in a better frame of mind. For Sergeant Rich, this is the preferable way to handle the situation, rather than disciplining an officer until they come into compliance, which is more the norm in the force. The worst thing the department can do, in his opinion, is exercise disciplinary process after a person has suffered a trauma. The department needs to appreciate what happened to the individual and help them get back in line where they belong.

Not only can an officer's job performance go into a downward spiral, but he or she may also end up dealing with substance abuse, depression, anxiety, relationship issues and potentially, suicide. Intervening at the right time—when a supervisor sees something that is completely out of character—and managing the situation are crucial to the officer's well-being. Supervisors need to offer the best help they can, or if they don't know how to handle what is going on they need to find somebody who does.

Supervisors have mechanisms in place within the department to send someone for help. They can make it mandatory that the officer attend therapy and get reports stating whether they have complied. An officer can be told that getting the appropriate help is a condition of their continued employment. It is ideal if the person goes of their own volition; but if everything else fails the supervisor can hold their job over their head. Hopefully this enables the officer to get seated in a room with the right person—someone impartial and non-threatening—and that person will get through to them. When somebody is there to sit and listen as you talk about the situation, you end up processing it, putting it in its appropriate place and coming up with a plan of action. The therapist may guide the conversation, but what it really gets down to is how the trauma is affecting the officer's life and the officer's relationships.

John had been left to handle the emotional repercussions of his shootings on his own. No one offered him any guidance. A few years later, after a major crisis involving someone from the State Police occurred, the State Legislature mandated the department to develop STOPS—State Troopers Offering Peer Support. The crisis involved an officer who was arrested for Driving Under the Influence. Had this program been in place, or had anyone recognized the warning signs and intervened after the officer in question received a D.U.I., he might not have fallen into a spiral of shame and despair, which resulted in his murdering his partner and committing suicide. Had someone noticed and understood the symptoms, a tragedy might have been averted. Officers, says Rich, have a moral obligation to help each other. Hopefully that will now be more forthcoming.

STOPS is staffed by 70 volunteers, master sergeant or below in rank, designated from each barrack and unit in the state. It is a union driven, state mandated program, with training provided by the Department of

Mental Health and Addiction Services and The Connecticut Alliance to Benefit Law Enforcement (CABLE).

For Sergeant Rich, being a peer support volunteer has been one of the most fulfilling aspects of his long career. He was a member of the steering committee for the program, which began in 2007. The program provides individual contact with officers, stress management and debriefing. Because Sergeant Rich was one of the guys in the field, he sees himself as battle tested. He's been through it. If he makes a recommendation, a trooper will listen.

In his twelve years in the Major Crime Squad he was involved in a multitude of critical incidents; murders of children, dealing with parents who lost children to SIDS, police involved shootings, and officers getting shot and catastrophically injured. "My experiences in the field help me to be a better resource," he said. "It makes me feel good that I am helping somebody else get through all this stuff, which I dealt with, marginally, on my own. Being a peer support person has been tremendously rewarding for me."

"A lot of us are cut from the same cloth as police officers. We're alpha dogs. We have to be able to handle ourselves and our business. We can't show any weakness. We're the people who, when all hell's breaking loose out there, need to be in control. That's what we do. So for someone with our mindset to actually let go of control and let someone else take the wheel for a little while, is tough. It's not something that a police officer can always do. That's why you see some guys bearing it alone, suffering in silence, and possibly using substances or having their relationships fall apart. All these things may happen because they can't get past the point where they think they're supposed to be tougher than this. In my opinion you're more courageous if you recognize what exactly is at stake and you say I am going to take care of this. That's courageous."

Sergeant Rich would like to see police officers place a greater value on their lives, their careers, and their relationships and ask for help when they need it. He believes it is crucial for officers to recognize what is on the line if they are not at their best—that the risk of not staying on top of your own mental health is that everything else is going to go down the tubes.

Patterson is also a peer support person and a great asset to the program. He brings instant credibility because everyone has an idea, to some extent, of what he went through, so they know that he understands. Because John went through hell, recognized that he was suffering from PTSD, and dealt with it, he is a role model of what to do. He can tell other officers, from firsthand experience, that what they are experiencing are normal human reactions to an abnormal situation. He can forewarn them about what might happen and what they can do to help themselves.

Sergeant Rich's experiences with John pushed him in the direction of getting better training in providing services to officers who are emotionally impacted by the traumatic aspects of their work. "I needed to be better at this. I'd be a better supervisor if I recognized these things. I really feel that it's been one of the best things I've ever done in my life and career. It's so needed for our people, especially us troopers. We have that image of being chiseled out of granite. Some days we are. We have to recognize what our people deal with and that some days we really don't have a choice. If the call goes out we go and that's it. So what happens afterward in terms of processing the incident is important."

Troopers can call Sergeant Rich for anything; it doesn't have to be a traumatic incident. They can call about their children, their relationships or their finances. STOPS volunteers are trained to recognize when something is beyond their capability to take care of, at which point they refer the officer to the Employee Assistance Program (EAP), which is run by an outside agency. Sometimes the volunteer has to strongly recommend that the person call the EAP. Sergeant Rich, for example, might tell an officer that he has the EAP number on his cell phone, "and by the way let me dial it for you." After the EAP has set up their services, the peer volunteer's job is to follow up by touching base with the officer. Depending on the situation, this might mean a phone call every day for a while, or every couple of weeks or months. A simple 'how are you doing' might be all the officer needs. The goal is simply to be available.

There are also times when an officer's buddy or supervisor will call and ask Sergeant Rich to reach out to the officer because they know something difficult is going on. He will do that, understanding that sometimes troopers, in the middle of their own life crisis, cannot see what is happening to them and need help to gain perspective. What might help them is a non-threatening, impartial call.

"Tonight I'm not a sergeant," Rich tells an officer. "I'm a Peer Support Volunteer and I'm going to listen to you. I'm not a supervisor.

I'm not discipline. I'm not an arm of the agency. I'm just a guy to listen to you, hear you out."

STOPS provides a personal, normalized experience for the officer in crisis. The caller is someone they can relate to as opposed to an unknown voice on the other end of the line; a person who is out there doing the same job; who understands what the officer is up against. It is a fellow police officer giving the recommendations.

"We are a long way down the road from John's situation," said Sergeant Rich. "We didn't know how to deal with him—I'm not saying it's anybody's fault—we always had some form of special services unit, but it really wasn't what he needed. He needed something else; the force needed to take the handling of his case away from the big brother aspect of the department. The disciplinary aspect of the department—beatings will continue until morale improves—does not work."

After the first shooting John and Jay were placed on desk duty. According to Sergeant Rich, an officer who has been involved in a shooting should not get placed on desk duty where they are handling emergency calls for help. The desk area at the barracks is chaotic— with a lot coming in all at once; 911 calls, trouble at the casinos and more. That is clearly not a healthy environment for someone already under stress, traumatized, and suffering from some kind of anxiety or PTSD.

At the time, Sergeant Rich was supervising Jay Gaughan. He would make it a point every night to go in and relieve Jay so he could leave the desk and do something else; get out and get a cup of coffee even. Rich would stay for two or three hours, until he was needed elsewhere. Putting these officers on the desk was not the way to handle things, but no one knew any better.

"What do you do with a guy you can't put on the road? That's what we do, we ride on the road. We could have, and we should have, done a better job with John and Jay and the other officers in similar situations. We owed it to them to do better, as far as I'm concerned," said Sergeant Rich.

He would like to see the department get to a place where every officer recognizes that they have a place to go. They are not there yet, but they are headed in the right direction. He also stressed the importance of troopers supporting one another. "Some cops believe that if you're not a cop and they don't know you, that you couldn't possibly relate to them and you're probably a scumbag anyway," he said. That's why STOPS is invaluable.

Sergeant Rich has never gotten to that negative place where he can only relate to other officers. He has friends outside of the department and outside interests. He says that his friends like to talk to him about his world and he doesn't mind talking some, but then they say, what am I going to tell you, that I made a big sale yesterday? There is little comparison in the day to day life of a police officer and that of any other professional.

Sergeant Rich hopes he never becomes jaded to the point where he can't sit down with someone and have a cup of coffee and talk. But he understands how that can happen to a trooper. Officers are subjected to a nonstop barrage of dealing with other people's lives and the horrendous things that they do to one another. "If you have a conscience you can't make peace with some of these things. So you have to get support and be there for one another," he said.

"John was involved in two shootings and he is still here. He probably could have gone out in some kind of early retirement if it got to that point, but he isn't ready for that. He's still got some gas in his tank. It was really my privilege to be involved with John through that time. And since we've parted ways work wise, every time I see him it's like coming home. There's a feeling of comfort, familiarity, trust all the way around. We can go a month at a time without running into each other, but I always love seeing him. He's one of those people I hope I'll always have contact with. He's always going to be burned into my mind."

Chapter 20

Let the dog maul him

I worked so many fucked up cases and saw so many deaths over the five year period I was with the Criminal Investigation Unit that my body and mind couldn't take it any longer. I decided I needed to go back on the road. My wife had always said that I became more depressed from seeing all of the dead bodies as a detective, than I had from both shootings. Maybe she was right. I was done waking up in the middle of the night freaking out, sweating and panting, wondering where I was and what was happening to me. I needed a change. Change would be good. Just what the doctor ordered.

By this point in my career it was hard for me to see any good in people when all I saw day in and day out was the bad things people did to each other. What's hard to understand is how my job made me hate people. When a police officer does something good for someone, it usually stems from something very bad having happened to them.

The road is what I enjoyed the most throughout my career. I enjoyed showing up while crimes were in progress. It was an adrenaline rush. It kept me young and kept my mind sharp. Being a detective, although extremely important, was like being a janitor; always cleaning up other people's messes. So I decided to return to the road.

Prior to leaving my house on the morning I went back to work in Jewett City, I got a call from my friend Jamie Chambers, who told me his wife Veronica woke up crying the night before because she dreamt I was shot and killed at work. In her dream I had gone to investigate an alarm at a car dealership and was shot and killed. The funny thing is that Winner Ford, where her dream took place, is located exactly half way between my two shooting locations. I asked him to reassure Veronica that I would be fine, and I could take care of myself. He told me to be careful. At this point I believed that I could survive anything God threw at me.

I jumped right back into my usual routine. If I didn't have any on-going investigations I would attempt to serve warrants or look for drug dealers and other criminals. Anyone who knew me knew I took great pride in the work I did and I was appreciative that I was recognized for my strong work ethic. I worked closely with my two partners, Keith Hoyt and Dave Lamoureux, to keep our people safe. Isn't that sad, I called the people of Jewett City our people. Take a drive through, you'll laugh.

Over the next three years, I continued to do my job as usual. I never went to an alarm at Winner Ford, and obviously wasn't maimed or killed as Veronica prophesized. I did however almost get my hat trick as they say in hockey (three goals in a game). One day as I was sitting in my office, a self-proclaimed Vietnam Vet came in and started rambling on and on about nothing. The guy was short, fat and had long hair and a beard. He looked as if he had just crawled out of a pig pen. When he left my office, I watched him get into an older, beat up, Chevy Celebrity with New Hampshire plates, and drive away. I ran the license plate and nothing came back. Over the next couple of days I saw the man driving his car around town and then he disappeared.

Ten days later he rolled through town while I was working the evening shift. He drove up and down Main Street, and in and out of business parking lots.

I pulled him over in the parking lot of a package store on Main Street. I asked someone to back me up because I knew this guy was a couple of beers short of a six-pack. As I was exiting my cruiser I saw that he was rocking back and forth in his seat, just like Joseph Parsons had done before the shooting. I drew my weapon and approached the passenger side of his car. From the looks of the interior, I could tell he was living in his car. There were clothes, food and papers everywhere. When I reached the front passenger door he stared at me blankly and started reaching for something underneath the papers on the front passenger seat. Déjà vu. I started replaying the second shooting in my mind which assisted me in handling this stop effectively. I wasn't scared at all. I was acutely aware of what I was about to encounter. I immediately opened the front passenger door and put my gun against the guy's forehead. While doing so I felt around the front passenger seat with my left hand and found a .50 caliber Desert Eagle underneath some newspapers. I advised my troop that I had someone at gunpoint, and when my backup arrived we took him into custody. It turned out the Desert Eagle was a pellet gun, even though it looked and felt as if it were the real thing. He was brought to Troop E and after determining he didn't have any real criminal history, was let go. I never saw him again.

Shortly after this incident, a former dispatcher at Troop E, Kurt Hall, was riding with me. Kurt was a Florida sheriff who happened to be here visiting his son, Doug Hall, who was a trooper at Troop E and worked up north with me in the Jewett City area. Doug had asked me if his father could do a ride along. Like most of my shifts, the night began very quietly and ended up being crazy. While at a rollover accident, in which the suspected drunk driver fled into the woods, the north patrols were dispatched to a domestic dispute in Sprague. This incident involved a man armed with a knife who had fled the scene on foot. Even though I was the resident trooper in Jewett City and was technically only supposed to handle calls within the town limits, I responded to the domestic. When I hear knife or gun, I want to be there. I need to be there. While driving to the domestic with lights and sirens, Kurt laughed because he knew that I would respond whether or not the dispatcher or desk trooper asked me to. Kurt and I had worked together for many years on the midnight shift and he could always count on me to be the first responder to every dangerous situation. Even if the situation was miles away, he knew I would respond to the scene until the problem had been taken care of by other officers, or I was called off by the dispatcher.

Two troopers responded to the apartment where the domestic took place to check on the female victim, while I located the accused down the road. He was sitting up against a guardrail directly across the street from the local watering hole—a dive bar really—The Stonehouse Café. The area was well lit and I determined the lighting was sufficient enough to handle the situation without using my cruiser's spotlight, which would probably have antagonized the man with the knife even more. I noticed both of the man's hands were hidden behind his back. With my right hand on my gun, I used my left hand to call the other units and advise Troop E I had located the man and provided them with my location. I asked the man to show me his hands. Before I could finish my sentence, he placed a large kitchen knife to his throat and told me if I came any closer he would kill himself. Even though in my mind I was thinking please God, go ahead and do it, one less piece of shit we'll have to deal with in the future, I told the man to drop the knife so we could find out what happened. Doug Hall arrived and advised the troop the suspect was holding a knife to his throat and requested a K-9 unit. Meanwhile, every low life from the bar had stumbled outside to find out what was going on. They all liked the show. It was their chance to get some air time on Cops or Real Stories of the Highway Patrol. Even though Doug and I had established a good rapport with the man holding the knife to his throat, we were unable to convince him to drop it. We even offered not to arrest him. We told him he could go for a nice ride in an ambulance to the hospital and we would call it a night—excuse my sarcasm. At least he was smart enough not to believe us. I kept my hand on my gun in case I needed to use it.

When the K-9 officer arrived, I waved him over for a conversation, deliberately within ear-shot of the man. I told the K-9 handler to get the dog out of the cruiser, and then when I knocked the knife out of the perp's hand with my nightstick, he should let the dog maul him.

As soon as the guy heard the word maul he threw the knife down the embankment behind the guardrail and turned around with his hands behind his back. We were able to place the accused under arrest with no further incident. The dog barking his balls off in the back of the cruiser probably sealed the deal. It would have for me!

After clearing the scene, Kurt told me how impressed he was with the way I had handled the event. Even though it was a volatile and dangerous situation, he commended me on how much compassion I showed for the asshole. That's why I think I'm a good cop. It's not about how smart a cop is, or how tough a cop is, it's about understanding people. That's the secret of survival—understanding the type of person you are dealing with, within the context of why you are dealing with them. It's that simple.

As soon as I saw the guy sitting against the guardrail, I knew that he didn't want to harm himself or me. Sometimes good people fuck up and have a bad day. I believed that this was one of those situations. I could tell by looking in his eyes and by his actions and words that he'd gone to great lengths to get himself help. That's why we handled him the way we did. Anyone of us could have taken our guns out, pointed it at the guy, and screamed at him to drop the knife or we would shoot him. But the situation didn't call for it.

A similar situation occurred on December 23, 2008. I was driving to my barracks for our Christmas luncheon when I heard over the radio that New London Police were following a vehicle on the highway. The undercover NLPD detectives had an arrest warrant for the passenger in the vehicle and they wanted a marked cruiser to pull the car over. Seeing that they were just south of the barracks, I screwed down the highway and pulled the offender's vehicle over on an off-ramp. The detectives pulled in behind me. As I exited my cruiser, I observed the wanted individual bending over and reaching toward the floor of the vehicle. As we approached the car, the passenger jumped out and ran down the snow covered embankment. Just as I was about to grab him, I saw him reach into his waist band. Knowing full well that he was trying to pull out a gun, I peeled off and ran side by side with him, pointing my gun right at him. I was waiting to see a little piece of the gun before I shot him. A split second later the detective tackled him like a lion tackling a wildebeest in the wild, and the fight was on. The asshole kept trying to pull the gun out of his waist band. With the help of other undercover officers, we ever so gently placed handcuffs on the offender with minimal force (that's a joke). When we stood him up, we found the loaded .380 in a sock underneath the snow. He had been lying on it.

When one of the detectives asked the idiot what he was trying to do, he replied that he was trying to pull the gun out so I would shoot him. Another suicide by cop. Just my luck. They laughed at him and told him that he was fucking with the wrong person. They were right. I told the kid that if I had seen the littlest speckle of his gun, he would have been dead, plain and simple.

Chapter 21

Real Stories of the Highway Patrol, Patterson style

From the start of my career I had a reputation as a gung-ho trooper. Real Stories of the Highway Patrol (RSHP) was a television series in the 1990s that capitalized on the success of "Cops." In 1995 RSHP chose the Connecticut State Police to ride with. For a few weeks that summer, the camera crew of the RSHP rode with troopers throughout the state, including Troop E in Montville, Connecticut, where I was assigned. Sergeants from the barracks had chosen a small number of troopers for the crew to ride with. While a few troopers showed the RSHP crew a good time, most of the troopers were not very aggressive and some of us feared that the Connecticut State Police would be perceived as a bunch of pussies by other state police agencies throughout the country.

During the time that RSHP spent at Troop E, troopers would tell the sergeants at "roll call" to allow the RSHP to ride with me. Everyone wanted to see what would happen if they did. One night the trooper assigned to the crew took the night off. When I got to roll call the sergeant was looking around the room for someone to assign. My buddies were pushing him to let them ride with John. At first I thought "no fucking way" because I didn't want to babysit two guys I didn't know. But then I thought they had a better chance of being involved in something with me, so I volunteered my services and the sergeant reluctantly agreed.

Off we went. As we were driving from the barracks to Jewett City I asked the crew if they had seen anything cool with the other troopers they had ridden with. They had, but nothing too crazy or serious. Within twenty minutes I pulled over a car in Griswold with an expired tag. A short time later I located narcotics in the car and was in the process of arresting the two individuals when Trooper Bowyer radioed that he was attempting to stop a car on 395 and was passing my location. I ran back to the car I had stopped, threw the drugs on the driver's lap and told him to wait for my return.

As I ran back to my car I looked at the RSHP crew and smiled. The funny thing was they were already smiling. They knew they chose the right person. We jumped on the highway and the race was on. I could see Bowyer about a mile ahead following the vehicle in question.

Bowyer radioed in that the person he was following had passed his cruiser at a high rate of speed, waved, and continued onward. Bowyer said when he activated his lights and sirens the person sped up and refused to pull his vehicle over.

I got my cruiser up to 120 mph just as we entered another troop area and had to switch radio channels. A few minutes later I caught up to Bowyer and entered the pursuit. Seconds later Trooper Jay Gaughan and his K-9 King joined the pursuit as well. I explained briefly to the RSHP camera crew why Bowyer was pursuing the offending vehicle and why I thought the person might be running from the police. I remember the crew asking each other if there was enough film in the camera to capture the pursuit.

As Bowyer continued to call out our location to the dispatchers and desk trooper, more and more troopers joined the pursuit. Technically there are supposed to be no more than three police vehicles involved in a pursuit at one time. For the sake of argument, let's just say that our numbers were slightly over the limit.

Every cop knows that a pursuit is like pole position in Nascar racing. You may be the lead vehicle in a pursuit in the beginning, then move to the middle or the back. But you're always trying to get to the front so you get a piece of the prize (I mean asshole).

At the beginning of this pursuit I was the second car. Once Jay and his K-9 arrived I let him go by me so I wouldn't get bit in the ass by King if the asshole stopped and tried to get out and run. So now I'm third. Jay's dog was fucking nuts. He had eaten the dashboard, doors and the headrests of Jay's cruiser.

As we screwed up 395, two troopers from Troop D jumped in front of the asshole's car, but somehow he got by them. So now I'm in 5th place (five is a good number to stop at). So I stayed at pole position #5 until we reached the Massachusetts state line.

Luckily there was no physical barrier at the state line, so we blew right through it. The RSHP loved filming the "Welcome to Massachusetts" highway sign at 100 mph. Less than a minute later I maneuvered my cruiser to the left of the assholes car and he tried to ram me. Okay. The crew didn't like that because I threw them around pretty good in the back of my cruiser.

Once we reached Exit 2 in Massachusetts the asshole decides to pull over in the center median. As I slowed my car to a screeching halt and opened my driver's door, the asshole threw his car back into drive and took off, heading back to Connecticut. At the same exact moment Jay rear ended my cruiser just as I closed my door and start driving again. Fortunately we didn't leave either of our cruisers' license plates in Massachusetts. So technically, we were never in Massachusetts.

Back onto the highway I was in 5th place. Based on my experience playing video games, in seconds I passed the offender's car and pulled in front of him. With the assistance of the other four cars (quietly laughing) involved in the pursuit we were able to stop the car. We slowly exited our assigned cruisers, patiently walked up to the driver's side car and politely asked him to exit the car. Then Jay's dog basically ripped the guy's triceps off of his arm as he was lying face down on the pavement. Then King bit two troopers on the ass and ripped Jay's pant leg off. All of which was caught on the RSHP cameras.

After clearing the scene I returned to Troop E to resume my patrol. While eloquently summarizing for the RSHP camera crew what had taken place, I was dispatched to a serious accident in Voluntown. As I approached the accident scene the operator of the involved vehicle was running away from the firefighters toward my oncoming vehicle. I was able to stop my car just in time to not run him over. He was arrested after a brief rest on the hood of my car.

By time we returned to the barracks, the RSHP camera crew was in disbelief. They kept saying it was the greatest night of their lives and how the producers in L.A. were going to love it. Realizing that several pursuit policy procedures were ignored I couldn't allow them to use the video, but Jay and I still have a copy of that eventful night. The next day the Commissioner of the Connecticut State Police reviewed the pursuit and kicked the Real Stories of the Highway Patrol out of Connecticut. I had the honor of being the last person the RSHP ever rode with in the Connecticut State Police. A few weeks later the producer of RSHP called and asked me if we had changed our minds about airing the video. The producers said that they wanted to use it for their "Top Ten" Christmas Special. Unfortunately it never aired.

Chapter 22

Come any closer and I will blow
my fucking head off

Twice as many police officers die by their own hand each year than are killed in the line of duty. In New York City alone it is estimated that 29 of 100,000 officers commit suicide every year, almost two and a half times the rate for the general population (12/100,000). Approximately one third of all police officers have Post Traumatic Stress Disorder (PTSD), diagnosed and undiagnosed; the majority of those officers will not go for treatment because of the stigma attached to seeking help.

But those are only the statistics. Instead of playing the numbers game, I'll tell you a story.

April, 2010. Another night driving around this little town looking for some asshole who is up to no good. The only thing I have to keep me awake is the fact that I'm listening to the Red Sox season opener against the Yankees on my radio. Don't worry, the Red Sox are winning.

Around 9:00 pm I stop some kid who is driving like Joey Chitwood down Main Street and pull him over. I tell him to slow down before he kills someone, 'cause I know what that feels like. After lecturing this idiot for a few seconds I slowly walk back to my cruiser, get in, turn my lights off and drive away, hoping he'd pay attention. I don't even make it a block when I hear the Troop E desk trooper giving a BOLO about a despondent female who is suicidal and armed and driving around the Montville and Preston area.

I turn my cruiser around, turn my lights and sirens on, and head out. While screaming down I-395 at one hundred plus miles an hour, the Troop broadcasts information that I don't want to hear. The despondent female is a cop who is armed with more than one gun and is possibly at the Mohegan Sun Casino. The whole time I am driving I keep thinking—great, a fucked up cop, drunk and armed at the second largest casino in the world. A shitty situation that probably won't end well. If I know one thing about cops, when they make a decision to do something, they do it, and there's no way anyone is going to talk them out of it.

Sure as shit while everyone is driving around the casino looking for her, casino security finds her vehicle and traces her to a gaming table on the casino floor. The good thing is we know where she is. The bad thing is she's carrying a knapsack filled with guns.

Just months earlier, a female trooper who I worked with at Troop E for many years retired, moved to Florida, and put a bullet in her head. I don't want this to happen again and in front of me, if I am unlucky enough to find her. I can't bear to think about what might happen, and hope someone else finds her. But guess who does?

You got it. As I drive out of the valet garage where her car was found I pass a female standing in a corner outside of the hotel. I hear her crying and arguing with someone on her cell phone. I know it is her because she has a knapsack on her arm. A heavy knapsack.

As soon as I stop my cruiser, get out, and call her name she puts her service weapon to the side of her head and screams, "If you come any closer I will blow my fucking head off." All the while she is drinking a $200 bottle of scotch and finger fucking the other guns in her knapsack.

While I speak and plead with her to reconsider her own death, I come to the realization that I may have to shoot and kill a fellow police officer. I have killed before in the line of duty, but killing a cop would be too much for me to bear. Luckily, on that night, she isn't ready to die.

Happy ending, right?

Wrong. Two weeks later she drives to New Hampshire, puts on her dress uniform, places a gun in her mouth and pulls the trigger.

Chapter 23

Return to my own land I shall not

"PTSD is a new name for an old story—war has always had a severe psychological impact on people in immediate and lasting ways... It's been with us now for thousands of years,"
Bentley, 1991.

Over the millennium, many terms have been used to describe this all-to-common and debilitating condition caused by war; combat fatigue, shell shock, battle fatigue. Historically, soldiers suffering psychologically from the impact of daily traumas were vilified with labels meant to shame them. For instance, in Great Britain during World War I, the Royal Air Force decided that combat veterans exhibiting symptoms of combat fatigue were "lacking moral fibre" and their records were stamped "LMF". During this time period, the British Army executed 306 soldiers for "cowardice" or "desertion".

During the Civil War, the military labeled the effects of battle on soldiers as Soldier's Heart or Exhausted Heart, names that may come closest to the truth of the experience. According to Bentley (1991), military doctors during the Civil War "diagnosed many cases of functional disability as the result of fear of battle and the stresses of military life. This included a wide range of illnesses now known to be caused by emotional turbulence, including paralysis, tremors, self-inflicted wounds, nostalgia, and severe palpitations." Often these soldiers held up during battle, but collapsed when they returned to the safety of their own homes.

Military doctors in Switzerland in 1678 were perhaps the first to recognize the impact of war on soldiers, and labeled it "nostalgia" (Bentley, 1991). This condition included feelings of melancholia, excessive longing for home, disruptions in sleep and appetite, anxiety, palpitations, fatigue, stupor and fevers.

Warriors in ancient times had their own names for it. Homer certainly understood it when he wrote these lines in the Iliad around 730 B.C.:

I would die here and now, in that I could not save my comrade.

He has fallen far from home, and in his hour of need, my hand was not there to help him.

What is there for me?

Return to my own land I shall not...I stay here by my ships a bootless burden upon the earth.

In Babylon, circa 1780 B.C., King Hammurabi wrote of "lost warriors", those who returned home from battle but left their souls on the battlefield. Ironically, Hammurabi ruled what is now modern-day Iraq where today 20% of returning veterans will suffer from PTSD or severe depression, and will be anywhere from two to seven times more likely to commit suicide than non-veterans.

Complicating this even more is the fact that the experience of combat troops in Vietnam, Iraq and Afghanistan differs widely from previous wars. While pre-Vietnam wars had their own particular horrors, those that followed have one critical element in common with police work. You don't know who the enemy is.

Like a firing range with pop-up targets, where some are gun-toting bad guys and others are moms holding children, the modern soldier and police officer both inhabit an environment where nothing is clearcut. There are no lines of enemy soldiers advancing in colorful uniforms. There are no distinctive enemy helmets, boots or armored vehicles.

Anyone may be carrying a concealed weapon. Anyone may be a lawbreaker, an insurgent, a thief or a killer. Anyone might be a peaceful villager, late shift worker, harmless senior citizen.

Whether it is Jewett City or Fallujah, daily living becomes a guessing game, with its own set of unique stressors. Before a shot is even fired, the cop and soldier both have to make thousands of split second decisions, assessing threats, deciding when to trust a civilian, or when to remain wary. Wary is easier, but it takes a toll. Wary is a good way to survive in an environment of threat, but a poor way to live your life. This form of hyper-vigilance, which is required to sustain oneself, is detrimental to one's mental and physical health.

Post Traumatic Stress Disorder can develop after a life-threatening event like military combat, law enforcement shootings, terrorist attacks, terrible accidents, natural disasters or violent personal assaults. Some survivors of these traumas return to normal given time. Others have stress reactions that don't go away and worsen over time. In England during the early 1800s, so many people were injured in accidents on the first steam locomotive lines that they coined the term "Railway Hysteria" for what the survivors felt after horrific crashes. After the Great Fire of London in 1666, people experienced nightmares, intense fear, anger, and feelings of discontentment. These people, like me, developed PTSD.

Individuals with PTSD are impacted in three general areas.

1) They have intrusive thoughts, which show up as either nightmares or flashbacks of the event.

2) They experience avoidance and numbing, which includes avoiding places that used to be enjoyable, or avoiding situations or conversations that are connected with the traumatic event.

3) They have increased anxiety and emotional arousal. They may have trouble sleeping, become irritable or angry, feel intense guilt or shame, be startled easily, see or hear things that are not there. PTSD is marked by physical and psychological symptoms such as depression, substance abuse or other addictive behaviors, problems with memory, difficulty making decisions, feelings of disconnection, difficulty prioritizing, fatigue, and relationship problems. My personal addictive behaviors of choice were gambling and eating. It's no fun.

There's a checklist for people who are most likely to develop PTSD. Top of the chart is those who experience "greater stressor magnitude and intensity, unpredictability", along with "greater perceived threat or danger". That's practically a job description for police officers and soldiers.

The American Psychiatric Association's current definition of PTSD includes two key elements.

1) A potential candidate for PTSD must have experienced or witnessed a traumatic event "that involved actual or threatened death or serious injury."

2) The response to this event must evoke feelings of "intense fear, helplessness or horror." In the 2013 edition of The Diagnostic and Statistical Manual of Mental Disorders, Fifth Edition (ESM-5), they will most likely omit the second condition of feelings evoked. In this new edition the proposed criteria state that "the person was exposed to one or more of the following event(s): death or threatened death, actual or threatened serious injury, or actual or threatened sexual violation, in one or more of the following ways:

▢ 1) Experiencing the event(s) him/herself.

▢ 2) Witnessing, in person, the event(s) as they occurred to others.

▢ 3) Learning that the event(s) occurred to a close relative or close friend; in such cases, the actual or threatened death must have been violent or accidental.

▢ 4) Experiencing repeated or extreme exposure to aversive details of the event(s). For example, first responders collecting body parts or police officers repeatedly exposed to details of child abuse (DSMV)."

For police officers, firefighters, emergency personnel or soldiers, the reaction to horrific scenes may not be immediate. They may appear calm and fully in control. This is a result of training and experience. Such professionals know they have to dissociate from emotions, or suppress them, in order to be able to endure the events they are called to. But the emotions are still there. Bottled up.

PTSD can manifest itself for months, or even years after an incident. And with soldiers and emergency personnel, there is always more than one traumatic instance to compound the situation. Individuals risk developing PTSD if they suppress their emotions after a traumatic incident and fail to receive or seek out professional support. This lack of support and understanding can lead to long-term emotional problems and negatively impact relations with others.

The U.S. Army, while not known for having the best record for treating PTSD, now offers several treatment programs, such as the Warrior Combat Stress Reset Program at Fort Hood, Texas. This multi-week program offers a variety of counseling and other support services.

Support programs for law enforcement are uneven. Police management may be more concerned with the appearance of providing counseling than actually doing it. Various jurisdictions of law enforcement agencies also may provide differing levels of support.

There were once treatment centers specializing in the treatment of PTSD for police and emergency personnel. However, the advent of HMOs and managed care forced most of those centers to diversify and treat many types of persons for addictions, depression and other mental health issues. There are still a couple of centers offering services only to emergency workers and first responders. One of those is On-Site Academy in Massachusetts.

If you're a civilian reading this, I hope it has given you some understanding of what law enforcement personnel go through. If you are a police officer, soldier, or any other kind of emergency services worker who may be exposed to events that can trigger PTSD, just remember you're not alone. There are a lot of people out there ready and willing to help, without judging you.

Let them.

Chapter 24

April and I

So where do I go from here? As I approach my twentieth year as a police officer I often contemplate what it will be like to go from one thousand miles an hour to zero the day I retire. The job, for most officers, is an identity; it defines them. That's why a lot of police officers lose their lives shortly after they retire. They are the ones who confuse their careers with who they are.

I'm not worried. I took this job because I could retire after twenty years of service. That was my plan from day one. My rationale has always been one of survival. It's been a tough road. I survived two deadly encounters. I didn't get divorced. I didn't become an alcohol or drug addict. I didn't commit suicide. Not bad for being the only trooper in the hundred and nine year existence of the Connecticut State Police to have shot and killed more than one person.

Luckily, I'm not a statistic. I have survived. Every year troopers are required to complete in-service training, 99% of which is bullshit. Every year we hear how many police officers commit suicide or get divorced. It's alarming. Google police divorce rates and suicide rates and learn what every cop already knows. The academy and most barracks have three-ring binders describing every police officer on and off-duty death, which they use as a learning tool.

Most people can't fathom the toll a twenty year law enforcement career takes on the body and mind. It's the reason I wrote this book and why it took me ten years to finish it. It was therapeutic to write my story. When I started psychotherapy, Dr. Hall suggested I keep a pad of paper next to my bed. When I had a dream related to my two shootings I could immediately write down what was playing in my mind. The first time I did it I couldn't stop writing. So here we are. If I can help one person by writing this book it will have made all of my hard work more meaningful and worthwhile.

There are so many stories I didn't write about that have negatively affected me. There's not enough time or paper to explain every scenario I've come across in the past twenty years. Don't get me wrong; not everything I've done or seen should be considered negative. I wouldn't have taken this job if it was not a rewarding career. The feeling of saving someone's life, returning a missing child to their parents, or having the producers of the Real Stories of the Highway Patrol tell you that you're going to be one of their all time, top ten shows, is indescribable. Solving a huge case and putting the "bad guys" in jail sustained me throughout my career and kept me moving forward through my dark times.

I'm sure my family, friends and coworkers think my two shootings are what define my career. They don't. The most important thing I've ever done on this job is to have a hand in the arrest and conviction of George Leniart for the kidnapping and murder of April Dawn Pennington. That's how I would like to be remembered by my brethren. It's funny. I think April and I were there for each other. When I was suffering through my gambling addiction and having frequent nightmares, I had her investigation to fall back on. When I needed direction in my life, I would focus all of my efforts on gathering information to put her killer away for life. Thankfully, he was.

Rot in hell you twisted motherfucker.

Sorry, I still have Tourette's. I'll try to work on that in retirement.

I've also come to the realization that in the next few months I will have to explain what I've been through to my 13 year old daughter and 11 year old son. My six year-old is not old enough yet. I have yet to figure out the best way to approach the subject.

For years my kids have asked me if I've used my gun or shot anybody. Shit, every kid I've come in contact with has asked me this question. The answer has always been the same, until now. I've explained to my kids that bad guys do exist and there are people in this world who like to hurt people. When my children were little and would wander away from my wife and me, I would ask them "do you want a bad man to take you?" This is definitely one of the things my kids hate about me. I always need to know where they are and I rarely let them out of my sight. Growing up I would say goodbye to my parents in the morning and not show up until nighttime. Other than saying I was riding my bike downtown, they had no idea where I was all day. This would never happen at my home. I will ask my wife where the kids are every few moments or physically check on them myself. The job has made me this way. I hope my kids will understand some day why I've acted this way since they were born.

For the last several years I have been considering my retirement options. My initial plan was to do twenty years as a Connecticut State Trooper, have the department pay for my master's degree during my last two years, then retire and become a teacher. One out of three isn't bad, I guess, especially since I've always hated school and have no desire to return to college and take more stupid, unnecessary classes. I've also come to the realization that I would probably be fired as a teacher within my first week for choking a mouthy student. I've also considered trying to get an investigative position at an insurance company, but I really don't want to work for a living anymore. Plus, the whole cubicle thing would weird me out.

I also fantasized about becoming a rodeo clown, crocodile wrangler, pet food tester, livestock masturbator, theme park vomit collector or a condom tester (XL, of course). Although I would probably excel at all of these jobs, except one, it would be too hard (ha-ha) to choose. Instead, I have applied to become a part-time police officer at a local casino. Hopefully I will be hired when I leave this shitty ass job.

Boy, I couldn't wait to leave that shitty ass job and retire.

On Tuesday, July 31, 2012, my buddy Stowell drove me to Connecticut State Police Headquarters to hand in all of my gear. Let's just say I had a big grin on my face. I really wanted to load all of my shit into my cruiser, set it on fire, and then crash it into the building, but instead I did the right thing. Still, it was a fun daydream.

Then we drove to a local bar and had a few cocktails (really a lot of cocktails) with friends, family and co-workers. It was a good night.

On Wednesday, August 1, 2012, I woke up and was no longer a Connecticut State Trooper. It was honestly no big deal. Having three shoulder surgeries and many months off after each one helped me prepare for staying at home. I wasn't only ready mentally, I was ready physically and spiritually as well to move on with my life. It was time to recharge my body, my mind, and my soul.

In the months since my retirement, I have had no regrets. I have not missed the job, just the guys and women I worked with. The only thing that has changed is my stress level. Although I have the same everyday stresses as everyone else, the police related stresses have disappeared, making my life more bearable and easier to handle. I am not thinking about shooting a third person, getting shot or being stabbed, seeing dead babies, burned bodies, viewing autopsies, or seeing a fellow officer injured or killed in front of me. That was a lot to deal with on a daily basis. Not to mention poor working conditions, crappy equipment, low staffing levels which lead to excessive workloads and inadequate support from supervisors and management. Hopefully, without all the pressures of the job, I will become a better son, brother, husband and father. Time will tell.

My wife threw me a kick-ass retirement party a few weeks later, which was attended by a couple of hundred guests. I never thought that many people liked me. It was funny. During the party my cop buddies kept telling me I can't fucking wait to retire. Their wives, on the other hand, asked how retirement was. I think their question was really for Wendy, and what was it like for her to have me home and out of danger's way. I think they also hoped that in retirement, the hatred their husbands developed toward humanity would change for the better. In my opinion, it won't. With enough time, it might diminish in intensity.

Most of my non-police friends and family members all said the same thing. You're the youngest retiree I've ever met in my life. I guess I'm the youngest retiree I've ever known too. Forty-two, not bad. But do you ever really retire? Nope. There's always the next job to go to, the bills still need to be paid, college still needs to be saved for.

The highlight of the night was when John Rich, my supervisor during those hard years in the Major Crime Squad, said a few words on my behalf. Like everything he says and does, it was perfect. During those awful years he understood what I was going through and provided me with all the support Wendy and I needed. If I needed time off, or needed to take a drive, I could do it without even asking him. He would call Wendy and check in with her to see how she and I were doing. Occasionally he would pull me in and we would talk about stuff that was happening in my life. As he was speaking at my party, it brought me right back to my feelings of him acting as my protector. That's why I, and everyone else, love him.

Then it was my turn. I'm sure most people thought I would thank certain people and acknowledge certain family members, which I did, but in a very different way. About two years earlier, when I was the Resident State Trooper in Sprague, Connecticut, I had thought a lot about my future retirement. Then one day I sat down at my computer and wrote a lengthy retirement poem that summed up my career. It took me twenty minutes to write it. Of course, it was quite good.

I was worried when the day came to read it, that I would not be able to get through it. I started out well, but when I got to the end, I couldn't read the last stanza. For some reason, unknown to me, when I started to explain how the department failed me, I began to have a very strong emotional reaction and I teared up. It was very emotional. Recognizing I would not be able to continue reading, my brother-in-law, Brian, finished it for me. Everyone loved it. Like this book, it is both dark and funny. Here it is, tears and all.

The Retirement Poem

I would like to thank everyone for coming to this great party
Especially my wonderful kids, Mia Eric and Aidan , and my
*   beautiful wife, Wendy*
To mom and dad for having me
To my three sisters Christine, Maureen and Tracy
And to the rest of my crazy family

As you can tell I didn't write a speech
I wrote everyone a poem
And as I'm reciting it I'll try not to scratch my scrotum

Here is a poem of my life in the CSP, and more importantly,
*   my life at Troop E*
I can assure you, it will be fuckin' funny
So make sure you pay close attention
Cause I'm ending my poem in true Johnny P fashion

I began my career in the 102nd Training Troop
Boy were we a fucked up group

After 7 months we were ready to graduate
I stood before my family and friends and was handed my fate
Troop E was announced and I was ever so happy
But my badge number was high and that was sort of crappy
Was it because I made my class and the instructors frown
Or because I was named class spectacle and class clown?

I then moved out east
To the bastardly beast
Known as Troop E

Troop E, Troop E
Who's better than we
The simple truth is
No one , really

The other troops call us names and say were too tough and
    mean
But deep down there jealous
Cause we're the best the CSP has ever seen
Be it a pursuit, a fight, or an armed robbery
There's nothing we can't handle
Just ask me

I started as a rookie and was told I was cocky
I wonder why, could it be, on my first day I told the sergeants
    to get their own coffee
I really don't know why people didn't like or understand me
Could it have been I was so polite or was everyone afraid I
    would call them a pussy

I began on the road and quickly moved to J.C.
Where the people have no teeth and they're all fuckin dirty
They were stuck in the eighties and couldn't read or write
But they had each other, and daddy made sure his little girl
    was not very tight

The Real Stories of the Highway Patrol showed up one day
The sergeant immediately put his head down and began to
    pray
Please don't let them ride with John he did say
Within ten minutes there was a pursuit from Griswold to
    Mass
Two people were arrested and more than one person was bit
    on the ass
We violated every pursuit policy in the A and O
But the Real Stories of the Highway Patrol said it would make
    their all time, top ten show
Once the head of the CSP learned and had seen what had
    happened
The Real Stories of the Highway Patrol were sent packin'

I did a long stint in the backroom
With a bunch of great guys who handled all the doom and
    gloom
There was Jr, Gates, Teddy, Steve, Jay and Mr. Waffles
And the rubber band fights were really not that awful
After going to the morgue and seeing sir shrek
My mind was snafu'd, so I went back north for another trek

To Sprague I went to clean up the town
Within a week they knew not to screw around
I arrested everyone who didn't fit in
That's because in my book everyone was committin' a sin
I've loved all the time I've spent on Pat 5
I can't believe I've driven through Appalachia and I'm still
    alive
Going from call to call was truly a blast
And I'm sad to say that this will be my last

I was at Troop E for many years, I did it all,
And because of it I even shed some tears
Thank god for my family, friends and peers
And to all the times we raised our beers

I went to the casino to make a little dough
Not bad for walking around lookin at all the ho's
All in all I had lots of fun
More importantly I helped put a huge dent in the state's slush
    fund
I'm sure this statement will upset my supervisors
But they were the dumbasses who took the test
And now have to work as janitors at Pfizers

During my career I've sent two to their grave
Some say I'm lucky, my family says I'm brave
But in the end I guess it doesn't really matter
Cause guess who's still here, pitter patter

So now that my career has come to an end
I wish everyone well until we meet again
#1323 to Troop E
31 I hope you'll miss thee

Know that my poem has come to an end
I'd like to direct my last comments to those who were afraid to
    attend
I gave this department more than they ever gave me
I've broken my wrist, my thumb and have had three shoulder
    surgeries
The physical pain will always come and go
But what this department has done to me mentally will always
    show
The so called support they've offered me throughout my career
    is a total "crock"
So the last thing I'll say as a trooper is the CSP can suck my
    cock.

Awards and Commendations

Over the years Connecticut State Trooper John Patterson has received repeated recognition, underscoring the important work he has done for his community.

1995 Mothers Against Drunk Driving Award (MADD)
1996 MADD
1997 Connecticut State Police Bravery Award
1997 Courage of Connecticut Award
1997 Top Cops Certificate of Nomination for Outstanding Achievement in Law Enforcement (Washington D.C.)
1997 Commissioner's Twenty (Top Twenty Shooter out of 1200 Troopers)
1998 Connecticut State Police Bravery Award
1999 Connecticut State Police, Troop E, Trooper of the Year
2000 Courage of Connecticut Award
2003 Connecticut State Police Unit Citation Award
2005 Connecticut State Police Meritorious Service Award
2006 Connecticut State Police Meritorious Service Award
2007 MADD Award
2008 MADD Award
2009 MADD Award
2010 Connecticut State Police Unit Citation Award
2010 Connecticut State Police Meritorious Service Award

The police are the public and the public are the police; the police being only members of the public who are paid to give full time attention to duties which are incumbent on every citizen in the interests of community welfare and existence.
Robert Peel (1788-1850), British Home Secretary and founder of the modern police force.

Dr. Henry Lee presenting John with
The Connecticut Bravery Award in 1998

Guidelines For Officer Involved Shootings

⯈ After my experience, and witnessing the follow-up of many other cases, these are the guidelines I believe should be put in place immediately at the scene of an officer involved shooting to more effectively assist the officer with the incident.

⯈ First aid should be rendered to any injured officer. If the officer is not physically injured, emotional support should be offered immediately at the scene. Allow the involved officer to contact anyone (family, friends, coworkers) they choose for support. Family members who wish to be with the involved officer should be allowed to do so if possible.

⯈ A union representative of the officer's choosing should be notified immediately and should respond to the scene. The union representative should explain the investigative process (Department's Criminal Investigation and State's Attorneys Investigation) and the administrative procedures (Internal Affairs Investigation) to the involved officer.

⯈ If your agency has a PEER Support program, the involved officer should be allowed to choose a Peer Support person to help them in the aftermath of the shooting. If the involved officer does not want a Peer Support person to assist them, don't push the issue. Provide the officer with the necessary information about the program and let them choose how involved they would like to be. Remember officers like to be in charge. Don't take that away from them.

⯈ Ask the involved officer if they would like to be removed from the scene or stay to assist investigators. If the involved officer would like to be removed from the scene allow the officer to choose a safe location to remain throughout the initial investigation. They do not need to go back to the police station and be placed in an interview room. That will only foster a feeling of wrong doing. If the officer would like to remain at the scene you should find a safe environment for the officer.

⯈ Allow the officer to contact and consult with an attorney if they choose.

⯈ Most departments will ask the officer to hand over any weapons that were used during the incident as evidence. A replacement weapon should immediately be provided to the officer. By no means should the involved officer be removed from the scene or remain on scene unarmed.

▷ Although officers should provide investigators with necessary and pertinent information to aid the initial investigation, officers should not be made to provide a formal statement right away if they are not ready to so. I found it beneficial after my two shootings to provide a formal written statement because I knew what I did was both legal and justified, and it was fresh in my mind. Other agencies allow up to a three day period before an officer is administratively required to provide a formal statement to investigators. Investigators should explain to the involved officers the benefits of providing an immediate statement or a delayed one.

▷ If the initial, at scene investigation determines that the shooting was justified, a department spokesperson should communicate this to all media outlets in direct support of the involved officer.

▷ The criminal investigation, State's Attorney investigation and the Internal Affairs investigation should be completed as quickly as possible. Progress reports should be given to the involved officer or officers weekly.

▷ The involved officer or officers should be able to stay out of work until all of the investigations are completed. This will assist in the psychological recovery of the involved officer and their family, as well as encourage a quick and thorough investigation. None of the officer's accrued personal time should be used during this period and the officer will continue to accrue personal time throughout the process."

▷ The involved officer or officers should be paid 100% tax free, as if it were a worker's compensation case. After my first shooting I was made to work the desk for three months and was unable to work overtime. Even though I was justified and was doing my job, I was punished financially by my employer.

▷ If any officer or dispatcher either witnessed or was directly involved in some manner with the incident, they should be provided a minimum of three days off. They should also be provided with Peer Support services.

▷ During the officer's time off, the department, the union, Peer Support personnel and the involved officer should work together to find a suitable duty assignment for the officer. The officer should remain in the assignment until he or she feels they're ready to return to the "road".

If the officer would like to remain in the agreed upon assignment, they should be offered this opportunity.

▭ Within one week of the shooting incident the involved officer should speak with a licensed mental health professional that has experience dealing with law enforcement officers. The involved officer and the mental health professional should determine if further meetings would be beneficial and/or necessary. Family members should also be offered mental health services.

▭ Mental health services should be paid for by either the department or workers compensation for the duration of the visits, until the involved officer, mental health worker, or family members decide treatment is complete. Access to mental health services should remain free throughout the remainder of the involved officer's career, as well as throughout retirement as symptoms of Post Traumatic Stress Disorder (PTSD) may reoccur at any time.

▭ If the involved officer is unable to return to full duty because of PTSD or is diagnosed with PTSD at anytime during their career, they should be allowed to retire with a full medical retirement.

Appendix 3

References & Resources

Bentley, Steve. January 1991. A Short History of PTSD: From Thermopylae to Hue, Soldiers Have Always Had a Disturbing Reaction to War. Retrieved from http://www.vva.org/archive/TheVeteran/2005_03/feature_HistoryPTSD.htm

DSM V—The Future Manual . Retrieved from http://www.psych.org/mainmenu/research/dsmiv/dsmv.aspx

EMDR Institute, Inc. Retrieved from http://www.emdr.com

International Society for the Study of Trauma and Dissociation. Retrieved from http://www.isst-d.org/sitemap/horizontal-menus/students-public-links.htm

International Society for Traumatic Stress Studies. Retrieved from http://www.istss.org/UsefulLinksAndResources.htm

Make the Connection, Shared Experience and Support for Veterans. Retrieved from http://maketheconnection.net/stories/story.aspx-?story_id=6&gclid=CPOq1LD2jK4CFYmK4AodjRV6eQ

MedLine Plus, A service of the U.S. National Library of Medicine National Institutes of Health. Retrieved from http://www.nlm.nih.gov/medlineplus/posttraumaticstressdisorder.html http:// www.policeptsd.com

PTSD Association Canada, PTSD Self-Assessment Checklist. Retrieved from http://ptsdassociation.com/ptsd-self-assessment.php

United States Department of Veteran Affairs National Center for PTSD. Retrieved from http://www.ptsd.va.gov/

Veterans; Statistics. Retrieved from http://www.veteransnewsroom.com/files/press/VETERANS-Fact-Sheet-Veterans.pdf

About the Authors

John G. Patterson, **Connecticut State Trooper**
John Patterson entered the State Police Academy in 1992, fulfilling his lifelong dream of becoming a police officer and continuing a multi-generational family tradition. During his twenty-year career he worked on the road for 14 years, as a detective for 5 years and in the Casino Unit for 1 year. Over the years he received numerous awards, including five Mothers Against Drunk Driving (MADD) awards, three Connecticut State Police Meritorious Service Awards, two Connecticut State Police Bravery Awards, a Top Cops Certificate of Nomination for Outstanding Achievement in Law Enforcement (Washington D.C.), two Courage of Connecticut awards and a Connecticut State Police, Troop E, Trooper of the Year award. He retired in 2012.
Website: http://JohnGPatterson.com

Deborah Mandel, **MA, LPC**
Deborah Mandel has been in private practice in southeastern Connecticut as a psychotherapist for three decades, and previously worked at a facility providing services for domestically abused individuals and rape victims. It was there that she received her first training in working with trauma survivors. Upon leaving the center and opening Chrysalis Psychotherapy Center, she continued her work with trauma survivors both individually and in group settings.
Website: http://chrysalispsychotherapy.com

James R. Benn, **Author**
James R. Benn is the author of the Billy Boyle World War II Mysteries, published by Soho Press. The debut title, Billy Boyle, was named one of the top five mysteries of 2006 by Book Sense and was a Dilys Award nominee. The eighth title in the series, A Blind Goddess, is a 2013 release. A former librarian, Benn lives in Hadlyme, Connecticut with his wife Deborah Mandel.
Website: http://www.jamesrbenn.com

Made in the USA
Charleston, SC
05 July 2013